LIVING
by the
FRUIT
of the
SPIRIT

ALSO BY DON M. AYCOCK

Eight Days That Changed the World:
A Devotional Study from Palm Sunday to Easter

God's Man: A Daily Devotional Guide to
Christlike Character (gen. ed.)

LIVING
by the
FRUIT
of the
SPIRIT

DON M. AYCOCK

kregel
PUBLICATIONS

Grand Rapids, MI 49501

For more information about Kregel Publications, visit our web site at www.kregel.com.

Cover and book design: Nicholas G. Richardson

Library of Congress Cataloging-in-Publication Data
Aycock, Don M.
     Living by the fruit of the Spirit / Don M. Aycock.
         p.   cm.
     1. Fruit of the Spirit. 2. Christian life. I. Title.
BV4501.2.A957   1999   234'.13—dc21   99-19009
                                                                        CIP

ISBN 0-8254-2003-2

Printed in the United States of America

1 2 3 4 5 / 03 02 01 00 99

To our sons, Chris and Ryan, who keep life hopping for us and who make living with them fun. They will be going to college soon after this book appears, and we already grieve that they will not be around as much. Much of what Carla and I know about love, joy, and especially patience, we learned from them.

And to our new family of faith, First Baptist Church of Palatka, Florida. May the fruit of the Spirit guide our lives as we get to know each other. Carla and I love you, too.

Contents

Introduction

When I was about ten years old, I went to the fair in a town close to where I lived. The variety of stomach-murdering food was a pure joy to a little boy who loved junk food. The booths with balloons for bursting and the stalls with BB guns for shooting out a star on a piece of cardboard were wonderful lures to make little boys spend their hard-earned quarters. But the most memorable attraction was the fun house. The fun house had walls of glass so you were not sure if you could go straight, and mirrors in one room that made you look at least seven feet tall. But the thing I remember most was the entrance. To get into the fun house, you had to walk across a bridgelike structure that swayed up and down and back and forth. If you could just get in, you would do fine.

In the years since my first trip to that fun house, I have thought often of the moving floor at the entrance. It seems almost like a parable about life. We try to do the best we can, but the very foundations under our feet seem to buckle and sway to throw us off balance. We might do well if it were not for the moving paths we travel. Our world has much that is good and beautiful, but it also has much that is ugly and harmful. At times the world itself seems very crooked. This presents a dilemma for Christians: How can we walk straight when most paths seem crooked?

The apostle Paul wrote his letter to the Galatians to help them learn what freedom in Christ is and appropriate that freedom as the anchoring force in their lives. In 5:22–25, Paul listed the fruit of the Spirit and urged his readers to live by the Spirit. He wrote: "But the fruit of the Spirit is love, joy, peace, patience, kindness, goodness, faithfulness, gentleness and self-control. Against such things there is no law. Those who belong to Christ Jesus have crucified the sinful nature, its passions and desires. Since we live by the Spirit, let us keep in step with the Spirit."

These elements of the fruit of the Spirit are precisely the steadying and energizing forces that help Christians walk and live in the present world. They have to do with our inner lives of faith and devotion, with our relationships with others around us, and with our love for the heavenly Father. As such, these matters represent some of the most basic of Christian ethics, values, and virtues. The elements grow inwardly and are expressed outwardly. Eugene Peterson has written, "God does not impose his reality from without; he grows flowers and fruit from within. God's truth is not an alien invasion but a loving courtship. . . ."[1]

Paul did not use the plural—*fruits*—here, but instead used the singular—*fruit*. I think he used the singular because he was not referring to many paths of the Spirit. He was giving a holistic view of spiritual life. A sound spiritual life will contain not some but all of these elements to some degree. It is like a hub with many spokes or a tree with many branches. The goal is to seek the fruit of the Spirit as a unified whole instead of as a fragmented, piecemeal vision.

A man appeared on the streets of Chicago a few years ago wearing a sandwich-board displaying these words: "Bad news! Bad news! The world isn't coming to an end. You're going to have to cope!" Those who live out of the power and values of the fruit of the Spirit can cope all right, but they will do more than that. After all, in Christ we are "more than conquerors through him who loved us" (Rom. 8:37). These basic aspects of faith help us to take whatever comes our way and transform it all for our betterment and the glory of God. One man expressed this hope in one of his prayers:

> Teach me, O God, so to use all the circumstances of my life today that they may bring forth in me the fruits of holiness rather than the fruits of sin.
>
> Let me use disappointment as material for patience.

Let me use success as material for thankfulness.
Let me use trouble as material for perseverance.
Let me use danger as material for courage.
Let me use reproach as material for long suffering.
Let me use praise as material for humility.
Let me use pleasures as material for temperance.
Let me use pain as material for endurance.[2]

An old proverb says, "Eagles don't flock. You have to find them one at a time." In one sense, this is true of Christian values. Finding them one at a time is what this book is all about. I have devoted one chapter to each of the elements that Paul mentions in Galatians 5:22 and have added an epilogue on walking in the Spirit.

The first chapter is on love. I have written about it intimately and personally because I think love cannot be explained adequately in the abstract. If you are helped through these efforts to live by the fruit of the Spirit, then my goal in writing this book will have been satisfied.

When God measures man, He puts the tape around his heart—not his head.

—Guideposts

Chapter 1

It Makes the World Go 'Round

L O V E

Learning About Love—A Personal Story

MY OLD '65 CHEVY PICKUP lunged forward as I headed home for the weekend. I was beginning my second year of college, and my time at school had been very difficult. I had come from a rural community and arrived on a campus with thousands of students. It was 1969, and the '60s atmosphere of wildness, rebellion, and general suspicion of everyone over twenty-one hung like a shroud over the large university campus. A shy kid from the "sticks" had a tough time ever feeling at home in a place like that. But others had done it, and, with all my seventeen years of enthusiasm still intact, I could see no reason why I could not make it, too.

The first year had come and gone, and I was entering my second year when the crisis hit me like a hurricane. The crisis, which was like what almost everyone else I knew was going through, was the question that haunted me like a ghost: *Who am I, and does anyone care if I live or die?* Many of my friends were going to Vietnam, and some of them were not returning. Others were heavily into drugs and, from the way they acted, might as well have been in Southeast Asia.

I was fortunate. The draft had not summoned me. Taking drugs had never interested me in the least. I attended a local church and even taught a youth Sunday school class. But all of that could not help quiet the question in my mind. It seemed like a dog growling in the basement. That angry, hurting, threatening question kept surfacing, and nothing could appease its ravenous appetite for long.

I dished out hors d'oeuvres of logic. "You know who you are. You are the son of Dewey and Mabel Aycock. You were born in Texas and lived most of your life in Evangeline, Louisiana. You worked on a rice farm and as a roughneck in the oil fields to go to school. You love music and the things of God." But these little appetizers did not last long. The dog in the basement kept growling its question: "Yes, but who are you, and does anyone really care?"

I also tossed out scraps of desperation. "Don't you know that everybody is feeling like this? Don't you realize that nobody feels perfectly right all the time?" But these scraps did not last long and were soon digested by that beast in the basement who never let up in its quest for an answer to its haunting question: "Who are you, and does anyone care?"

I was not taken by surprise, then, when the crisis came. It was no thief in the night, slipping silently into my dormitory room to carry away my few precious belongings. It came instead as a masterful landlord who pounded on the door to demand immediate and respectful admittance. I knew that sooner or later I had to answer that knock, but I would have liked to put it off as long as possible.

When I headed my old Chevy pickup home for that weekend, it was for no sock-washing. It was for a reunion with a part of me that had been left behind. I do not know how my truck stayed on the road. I cried all the way home with an incredible realization of the answer to my question: "Who am I?" The answer came this way: "I am my parents' son. I am growing and maturing and realizing the answer to the second question—'Does anyone care?' The answer is an undeniable, unswerving, absolute 'Yes!' Someone does care. I am loved." I was not going crazy that afternoon. I was going sane.

This answer had always been part of me. I had always known it, but there are times, such as going off to college or work, when a person needs to feel loved. Sometimes the distance between the head and the heart is more than a matter of eighteen inches. It is sometimes measured by the yardstick of years of struggle and pain and doubt and by the ruler of regret.

Driving home that fall afternoon gave me a chance to reflect on my life. Various images displayed themselves on the screen of my memory, and I watched the show with amazement. I was no casual observer but rather the cast, the director, and the stagehand.

I saw a little boy of seven or eight come walking into the living room with his BB gun slung over his shoulder. As he passed in front of the old Zenith black and white TV, the BB gun went off and shot out the picture tube. Panic and fear seized him, and he was sure his parents would, too. Instead, they sized up the situation and peered into the face of a terrified little soldier whose world seemed to have shattered along with the picture tube. A loving mother and father decided then and there that their little boy was worth far more than an old Zenith. They assured him that it was not his fault and that the BB had not even come close to the TV. It just "happened" to explode about the same time as the boy passed in front of it. To a terrified seven or eight-year-old kid, such an explanation seems perfectly logical, and he happily accepted it as the true account of the death of the TV. Only later did he figure out what really had happened and why his parents "stretched" the facts a bit. That feature presentation played in my memory that fall afternoon and went into reruns many times later. "I am loved."

The second feature came on. It showed that same boy, now a bit older—about ten or twelve. He was in a Texas oil field where his father was a toolpusher (the foreman on a drilling rig). A truck from a chemical supply company came lumbering down the board road on its way to the drilling site. The driver turned around and began backing up to the supply house. He could not see everything clearly and backed his truck into the radiator of one of the large diesel engines used to pump the drilling fluids. The truck driver stopped when he felt the bump and jumped out to see what had happened. He saw the boy standing there watching the accident. The toolpusher came running over.

Before he could say a word, the truck driver said, "That kid over there was in my way. I didn't want to run over him, so I had to swing around him. That's why I hit the pump. It's his fault."

The boy was stunned. But before he could think to speak, he saw his father get red in the face and get right up into the face of the driver. He yelled over the roar of the rig noise, "I saw exactly what happened. He was standing over here way out of your way. He didn't have anything to do with it. You're just a bad driver who just tore up my radiator. It's *your* fault and your company is going to pay for getting it fixed. Got it?"

The driver just nodded, pulled his truck out of the pierced radiator, and unloaded his supplies. Later, the toolpusher took the radiator to a shop to have it fixed, and the boy went along. He told his son, "I know that wasn't your fault, so don't worry about it. And if anyone ever tries to blame you for something like that again, you come tell me. We'll get it straight in a hurry."

Parents sometimes overprotect their children and never let them live up to the consequences of their own actions. Others always assume the worst about their kids, blaming everything on them, even if it was not their fault. My parents knew the difference, and that day in a Texas oil field many years ago is riveted to my memory. "I am loved."

Other little films played themselves for me that afternoon as I headed home. Vignettes long packed away in storage bubbled to the surface as if on their own. I saw a father standing behind his son, with his arms draped over the boy's shoulders and making a "V" across his chest. He proudly told his associates at work, "This is my son." Both the boy and the man beamed. I reviewed the scene of parents presenting their son a brand new Bundy trumpet in the eighth grade because he wanted to be a musician. New trumpets cost a lot of money, money that came hard. But they cared about what their son cared about. I watched the rerun of a father giving his little boy a guitar and always requesting in later years, "Hey, get your guitar and play us a tune."

Many other images came. The boy and his brother and father made a wooden boat to fish in Bayou Des Canes and spent many joyous hours hauling in bluecats off a trot line. I saw the boy out in a garden working side by side with his father. He hated planting a garden, but he liked working with the older man. Is it any wonder that the replaying of those memories, along with many others, had a healing effect on me as I struggled to ask the perennial teenage question?

But there are memories of a totally different kind, too. I look back on times when my father worked away from home, and I missed him and longed to talk to him. But all of these scenes have little power to affect me now because the ones in which I felt loved, appreciated, and accepted dominate my mental and emotional landscape.

Truly, love is a healer of all manner of human hurts. Even medical research is discovering this truth. In his book *Love & Survival: The Scientific Basis for the Healing Power of Intimacy,* Dr. Dean Ornish wrote, "Love and intimacy are at the root of what makes us sick and what makes us well, what causes sadness and what brings happiness, what makes us suffer and what leads to healing. If a new drug had the same impact, virtually every doctor in the country would be recommending it for their patients. It would be malpractice not to prescribe it. . . ."[1]

This wise physician realizes that love, or the lack of it, affects us in positive or negative ways, but it is never neutral. For people who have read the Bible, that news comes as no surprise. Why? Because, as 1 John 4:16 puts it, "God is love. Whoever lives in love lives in God, and God in him." Let us explore this idea further.

Love and God

A theologian wrote, "To love always implies personal investment in the object of love; where there is no evidence of such personal caring, one may question love exists for the object."[2]

Personal investment. That is a good phrase. That was God's choice in dealing with mankind in love. That is what the Cross is. Many people know that the original language of the New Testament is Greek. In that language, three words are primarily used for love:

1. *philia:* love for one's fellow human being—care, respect, compassion;
2. *agape:* our love for God, a reverence for the divine being of God; and
3. *eros:* affectionate, tender hungering for union with the loved one; passionate desire for a fulfilling relationship.

Which of these terms best describes God's love? The normal answer is the second word—*agape*. But the truth is that God's love is all three terms—and more.

When Paul referred to the fruit of the Spirit as love, I feel sure that he had many things in mind. He meant primarily that astounding love that God has for His children. To speak of the love of God is like speaking of the universe. I cannot even imagine it, so I will have to do what scientists do with the universe—break it down into smaller parts. They speak of galaxies, such as the Milky Way; of individual planets, such as the Earth; of specific countries, such as the United States; of unique states, such as Tennessee; of definite places, such as Memphis; and of specific individuals, such as me.

First John 4:7–21 is one of the most amazing passages in the entire Bible. It begins and ends with the affirmation that love is from God from first to last. "God is love." This is a far cry from the "unmoved mover" or "that, than which nothing greater can be conceived" of the philosophers. Because God is love, I am. I exist through the goodness of His letting there be life. He spoke the eternal word, "Let there be light" and there was light. Similarly, God said, "Let there be Don," and there was Don! God expresses His love through His letting be. He lets people and plants and an entire universe be. This letting be calls persons into existence and leads them on to reach the full potential of their lives. God confers Himself in the lives of those who welcome Him. He sustains life and perfects its creative possibilities. We are because God lets us be, and He lets us be because He is love.

This gives us a clue to the meaning of life and the Christian faith. God, who created all things and creatures, did not find supreme pleasure in them until He created people, who, like God, can love and be loved. It is thus while I love and allow myself to be loved that I am most like God. Piety does not mean that I "play God." It means that I allow myself to live in the relationship for which God most completely fit me, namely, love.

In his classic book on biblical love, *The Greatest Thing in the World,* Henry Drummond looked at 1 Corinthians 13 as *the* passage that best describes and defines love. Drummond said that God-given love as there described has nine ingredients, which he charted as follows:

Patience	"Love is patient."
Kindness	"Love is kind."
Generosity	"It does not envy."
Humility	"It does not boast, it is not proud."
Courtesy	"It is not rude."
Unselfishness	"It is not self-seeking."
Good Temper	"It is not easily angered."
Guilelessness	"It keeps no record of wrongs."
Sincerity	"Love does not delight in evil but rejoices with the truth."

In a new edition of Henry Drummond's book, Lewis Drummond noted the similarities between the qualities of love in 1 Corinthians 13 and the fruit of the Spirit in Galatians 5:22–23.[3]

1 Corinthians 13	Galatians 5:22–23
Patience	Patience
Kindness	Kindness
Not jealous	Joy
Not arrogant	Gentleness
Not counting evil	Self-control
Not provoked	Peace
Holy	Goodness
Selfless	
Enduring	Faithfulness
Humble	

The fruit of the Spirit grows out of love.

Francis de Sales (1567–1622) wrote a devotional guide titled *Introduction to the Devout Life* in which he reflected on the love of God and the need of people to love Him. He thought that God wants the love of people as expressed through their devotion to him. He wrote: "True devotion . . . presupposes not a partial but a thorough love of God. For inasmuch as divine love adorns the soul, it is called grace, making us pleasing to the Divine Majesty; inasmuch as it gives us the strength to do good, it is called charity; but when it is arrived at that degree of perfection by which it not only makes us do well but also work diligently, frequently, and readily, then it is called devotion."[4]

God's love can be conceived in an abstract, detached way, but I really think that de Sales was right in thinking about it in personal and intimate terms.

I wrote at the beginning of this chapter about a spiritual crisis that changed my life. God, in His love, uses such crises to communicate His care. That is what Easter Sunday is. That is what any crisis of separation is, whether it be death, a divorce, a child leaving home, or some other event. During those times when we have to look our solitude squarely in the face, we find that the face is friendly. God is there because God is love.

First John 4:18 says, "There is no fear in love. But perfect love drives out fear, . . ." God frees me to love myself, knowing full well that I am far from perfect but still okay. He frees me to love my family, even though my love is not fully mature and they do not fully respond to me. God frees me to love my friends, even though they sometimes disappoint me and I betray their trust. God, in Christ, comes to me with an offer of eternal love. I can refuse only at my own peril. "But perfect love drives out fear, . . ." So I am open to God's love as I am open to a friend or my beloved wife and children. It is here that I find myself "at home" in His presence, accepted as His child, and protected as His precious creation.

Love and Marriage

Growth, change, and healing come not only from parental and divine love but also married love. Many a person who has felt unloved in youth has learned to be loved and to feel loved later in life by losing himself or herself in the life of another. Jesus was right when He said, "For whoever wants to save his life will lose it . . ." (Matt. 16:25). This means to enter so deeply into the life of another that I am no longer the center of my universe. This happens spiritually in Christ. It also happens emotionally in marriage.

Some people are heralding the death of marriage, but such proclamation is greatly exaggerated. Men and women will always learn to care for each other. The survival of humanity depends on it, although procreation is by no means the primary reason for marriage.

My discovery of the wonder and mystery of losing myself in the life of someone else came, like many of life's good things, unexpectedly. My wife and I met in an unusual way but chose each other. Carla and I have celebrated our silver anniversary of married life. We are the parents of twins, Ryan and Christopher, who are growing up to be great young men. How can I refer to any of that as planned, logical, or ordinary? Yet, in its own way, this is exactly what it is. Our story is unique in its details, but many, many people have had similar experiences of love. People who at first did not even like each other later ended up "hitched." In the case of a couple who are friends of ours, the man was the woman's high school teacher. Later they married and are today one of the strongest families I know. Another couple began their relationship with the man being the woman's supervisor in a hospital laboratory.

I have experienced nearly indescribable support in my marriage. God did not make a mistake when He set lonely people in families. Psalm 68:6a puts it this way: "God sets the lonely in families." When Adam first saw Eve, he exclaimed, "At last!" (see Gen. 2:23–24). He knew a good thing when he saw it.

But there is great confusion today about what love is. I recently did an internet search using the word *love* and came up with more than twenty-two thousand references! The very first one was pornographic, and the rest were widely diverse. Some of the topics that came up under *love* included romantic poetry, tourism slogans (e.g., "I Love New York"), pictures purporting to display love, an essay on love and hate in the work of Tennessee Williams, love songs, adoption services, places that sell "love potions," pen pal services, dating services, on-line love tips, and some guy in Canada who writes that he is God and created the world.

Love, as Paul put it in Galatians 5:22, is a fruit of the Spirit. This does not mean that it is some abstract, bloodless, lifeless principle. The love between a man and a woman in marriage is as much the work of God as is the love of God for mankind. Both are theologically oriented. A church is the proper place for weddings if at all possible. The building and the surroundings say symbolically, "There is a third party involved in this union. He is the same One who said, 'Let there be light' and 'Let there be love.'" And behold, there is both!

The importance of love in marriage is demonstrated by the following situation. Joseph Stalin was the leader of the Russian communist revolution after the death of Lenin. He was married to a woman named Catherine Svanidze. Stalin seems to have loved her deeply. When she died at an early age in 1907, Stalin pointed to her coffin and said, "She was the one creature who softened my heart of stone. She is dead, and with her have died my last warm feelings for humanity." He pointed to his heart and said, "It is all so desolate here, so inexpressibly empty."[5] Stalin went on to rule one of the most repressive, bloodthirsty regimes ever known. He is responsible for the deaths of an estimated twenty million of his own people! I have to wonder what would have happened had his wife lived so that her love might have continued to soften Stalin.

Love and Friendship

We cannot think of love without thinking of friendship. These two concepts are closely related. But when was the last time you read something about friendship? You can find mountains of books on love, but the pickings for friendship are pretty slim. Even when someone tries to do something with it, misunderstandings crop up, especially with friendships among men.

When Stuart Miller began research for his book *Men and Friendship,* most people thought he was working on a book about homosexuality.[6] But Miller was asking the question many men raise, "Why don't I have many close friends?" After spending years searching for answers, he concluded that genuine friendship is hard to find.

"True friendship," he wrote, "must also be true engagement with the friend—a very frequent mutual holding in the mind and heart. Though the centrifugal pressures of modern life limit the frequency of the physical presence of friends, engagement makes physical proximity less of a problem. Male friendship can thus be thought of as a place in a man's inner being, a space in his life, that is daily occupied by another man, a place that is regularly charged with love, concern, hurt. *Engagement* means emotional involvement."[7]

The rise of groups such as Promise Keepers is, in part, the result of men wanting more out of life and relationships than just golfing buddies. They want close relationships with other men. They want love and friendship.[8] In his *Confessions,* St. Augustine wrote, "Men go forth to wonder at the heights of mountains, the huge waves of the sea, the broad flow of the rivers, the vast compass of the ocean, the courses of the stars; and they pass by themselves without wondering."[9]

To wonder means to accept ourselves and our full capacity to love others and to express that love. That is often difficult to do. We fear that we might appear weak or foolish to others if we open ourselves to love. But what other option is there? To remain suspicious and nonloving?

Evelyn and James Whitehead have written of our need to learn to express love in friendships and other ways. They write, "The Christian injunction to love one another, for example, is complemented by learning how to express and engender this love. Loving entails more than good feelings or proper attitudes; it involves certain behaviors—sharing of myself, empathy with others, confrontation. . . . To share myself with another, I must be psychologically disposed, able to overcome the hesitancy suggested by fear or suspicion or shame. But, these overcome, I must be able actually to share—to disclose myself in a way that is appropriate for me and for the situation."[10]

When I was growing up, I had many friends but one special one. His name is Milton. He and I were almost inseparable. We lived a half mile apart in a rural area of south Louisiana. There were woods, swamps, a bayou, and pastures for cattle around us, and we knew every square inch of them. Together, Milton and I hunted, fished, went to school, played basketball at school and softball at home, and threw cow "muffins" at each other. We once lined up tin cans on the little road in front of our houses so cars would have to slow down when they got there. We waited in the palmetto bushes and shot out their tail lights with BB guns. (I've regretted this many times since!) We swung from vines out over Bayou Des Canes, giving our Tarzan yells as we let go and hit the water. We climbed small pines, grabbed the tops of these saplings, and jumped out so the trees bent and we got an "elevator" ride down. Sometimes the tops snapped off, and our ride down was faster than we wanted! Milton and I picked mayhaws in the swamps and rode around in boats during flood times. He had a huge abandoned sawdust pile behind his house, and we spent many hours tunneling through the sawdust with old stockings over our heads to keep the sawdust out of our eyes and noses. We were friends, and friends will do anything with—or for—friends.

Milton and I do not see each other very often now. We have gone our separate ways as adults do, although I still hold him in high esteem. There is something about that relationship that taught me some important things about friendship.

Friends have time for each other. This sounds like an obvious truism, but think about it for a minute. If you are "average" (whatever that means), you probably would like to have more friends, especially those who are willing to spend time with you. I am not referring here to a next-door neighbor who drops in unexpectedly to take up your precious time with idle chatter over coffee. Instead, I am thinking of a close friend who enjoys the same kinds of things you do, whether it be spending the afternoon in front of the TV watching a football game, going shopping (my wife's favorite hobby!), snagging a few bass out of your favorite honey hole, or traveling to some unusual destination for a day's enjoyment.

I have a friend named Bill who was in seminary with me. He and I shared a common interest—goose hunting. We spent many hours together nearly freezing to death in a goose blind on the Ballard County Wildlife Refuge in LaCenter, Kentucky. I am not sure about Bill, but I went hunting not so much for the meat as for the fun and diversion. We would tell every joke we knew and laugh more than I can tell. Somehow stories seem funnier when you are in a pit below ground in twelve-degree temperatures with sleet and snow falling. To this day, I do not know how we ever got any geese. Surely they could hear us a half mile away, but we almost always went back home with game. I have not gone goose hunting in a long time, and I miss those times of hilarity in a goose pit.

Friends make time for each other, not only for the fun times but also for the tragic times. I will never forget when a close friend showed up at my office. He looked haggard, and when I asked what was wrong, he explained that his wife was in the hospital because of a suicide attempt. Nothing in the world could have gotten me away from him that afternoon. There have been times, too, when I really needed to talk to a friend. I am glad for people who make time for me, and I try to do this in my work. Pastoral care is intensified friendship carried on by a man or a woman willing to listen—really listen—and then offer insights and support.

Friendship comes through people being open with each other because without openness, close relations cannot develop. If I go about my life as if I were somehow totally self-sufficient, and therefore closed off to others, then I would have no friends. When I display an attitude of openness with everything in my life, from words to deeds, I then invite others to get to know me. Friendship wears a welcome mat on its face. The strange thing about it is that if a person intentionally tries to make friends, he sometimes succeeds in driving people away instead of bringing them close. We cannot make someone like us. We can only be available to allow a friendship to develop.

Thomas Lea described love as "triumphant good will toward others."[11] That describes perfectly the biblical picture of love— love of God for mankind, love of husband and wife, and love of friends for each other. Real people with real problems need real relationships. That is why love is so necessary. For example, pastors are not God, and we do not want to be treated as such. We want to be included as real people. That's why I get together with a small group of fellow pastors regularly. The first letters of our names together are DSTERB. That is a perfect name for our group. We're probably disturbed! All of us were in the doctoral program together in New Orleans. We love being together for fellowship, study, great food, and plain fun. We get together three or four times each year for a study session in which we research a topic or review books or talk to some expert. Aside from the technical information I receive from these men, I think of them as my friends whom I love. I could tell them anything and still be accepted. We keep in touch by e-mail and phone.

Friendship gives itself away. Every true friend I have is one who is willing to give himself or herself to me in trust and mutual protection. When I was the pastor of a church in Kentucky several years ago, we had several seminary students working with us in various capacities. When Carla and I got ready to leave that church, two of the students, Reid and Jean, gave us a copy of the children's book *The Velveteen Rabbit*. They marked a place in the book that was a conversation between the Skin Horse and the Rabbit. The conversation goes like this:

> "What is REAL?" asked the Rabbit one day. . . . "Does it mean having things that buzz inside you and a stick-out handle?"
>
> "Real isn't how you are made," said the Skin Horse. "It's a thing that happens to you. When a child loves you for a long, long time, not just to play with, but REALLY loves you, then you become Real."
>
> "Does it hurt?" asked the Rabbit.
>
> "Sometimes," said the Skin Horse, for he was always truthful. "When you are Real you don't mind being hurt."
>
> "Does it happen all at once, like being wound up," he asked, "or bit by bit?"
>
> "It doesn't happen all at once," said the Skin Horse. "You become. It takes a long time. That's why it doesn't often happen to people who break easily, or have sharp edges, or who have to be carefully kept. Generally, by the time you are Real, most of your hair has been loved off, and your eyes drop out and you get loose in the joints and very shabby. But these things don't matter at all, because once you are Real you can't be ugly, except to people who don't understand."[12]

Jean and Reid were saying to me and Carla that this is what we had done for them. They wrote as their inscription, "To the Aycock Family—A Real family which possesses the gift for helping others to feel Real." I treasure those words, and I have often gone back to that passage in the book. It says something so intensely personal. I have taken it as a sort of model for what I want to be to others in my friendships. I cannot be this to everyone because not everyone wants it. But to those who do, I am willing to try to offer it. Only love can make for good friendship. Francis Bacon was right when he said of friendship, "It redoubleth joys, and cutteth griefs in halves."

Love—it not only makes the world go 'round but also makes the trip worthwhile.

Joy is the echo of God's life within us.
—Joseph Marmion

Chapter 2

Joy to the World
J O Y

LONG BEFORE "JOY TO THE WORLD" was a Christmas hymn, it was the insignia of the Christian church. Joy was the mark of those faithful men and women of antiquity who faced persecution with the stamina to overcome it and problems with the strength to conquer them. Paul called his friends to a life of joyful living that, as the fruit of the Spirit, enabled them to withstand anything. Consider this counsel: "Be joyful always; pray continually; give thanks in all circumstances, for this is God's will for you in Christ Jesus" (1 Thess. 5:16–17). The list is headed by joy. There is a lesson here.

The New Testament uses eleven basic words associated with varieties of joy: exultant joy, gladness, pleasure, courage, hilarity, boasting, blessedness, optimism and enthusiasm, inward joy, leaping for joy, and shared joy.[1] The last three of these terms are most important for our purposes here.

Leaping Joy

Sometimes life is filled with the glory of God, and we see grace in each face. Joy comes bubbling to the surface, and we feel like jumping for joy. This emotion was not invented by kids on Christmas morning. As far back as we can remember in our religious faith, people have expressed their joy through movement. David danced before the Lord, even if his wife did think he had lost his mind (see 2 Sam. 6). Luke tells us that such joy is a light, skipping movement. When Mary visited Elizabeth before the birth of either of their children, Elizabeth said, "As soon as the sound of your greeting reached my ears, the baby in my womb leaped for joy" (Luke 1:44). In Bunyan's *Pilgrim's Progress,* Christian experienced forgiveness at the cross, and then, "Christian gave three leaps for joy, and went on singing."

Robert Burns wrote a poem in which he expressed his feeling that an alehouse was a warmer, more inviting place than a church. I do not know much about alehouses, but I do know something about churches. And as much as I hate to admit it, Burns is right in pointing out that a church can be a cold, ominous place. But it should be the focus of life and warmth, of laughter and mirth, of deep feelings expressed in significant actions. Most of all, the church should be a place of joy where people worship God with a sense of anticipation and quiet enthusiasm. How unbiblical is a drab, yawning, lethargic group of people who have dragged themselves out of bed and to the service, and who think about everything except the fact that they have more right to a leaping joy than anyone else on earth!

As I think back about some of the people I have known, I remember some who have reflected such joy. There is the woman who simply smiles at church. This seems so trivial, but as I scan the faces poised toward me on Sundays, I realize that her joy-reflecting smile is anything but trivial. There was a man, now dead, for whom life was a celebration instead of a wake. He simply could not help living as if life were a kind of perpetual circus, because for him it was. God did not make some sort of ghastly mistake when he gave us the gift of life or renewed life in Christ. We can leap for joy—the sheer joy of knowing Christ and being known by Him.

Inner Joy

Another sort of joy is described in the New Testament. It is an inward sort. The word *rejoice* comes from this origin. Paul used it as an imperative: "Rejoice with those who rejoice . . ." (Rom. 12:15). Also, he promised this joy to those who are filled with the Spirit: "May the God of hope fill you with all joy and peace as you trust in him, so that you may overflow with hope by the power of the Holy Spirit" (Rom. 15:13).

Jesus spoke of this inner joy as reflecting the feeling one has over the lost coming home. He said, "I tell you, there is rejoicing in the presence of the angels of God over one sinner who repents" (Luke 15:10). The father in the parable of the lost son says to the older brother, "But we had to celebrate and be glad, because this brother of yours was dead and is alive again; he was lost and is found" (Luke 15:32).

Strangely and almost inexplicably, inner joy is sometimes related to suffering. To say that joy and suffering go together seems like saying that matches and dynamite go together. But this is precisely what the New Testament affirms. Peter said, "But rejoice that you participate in the sufferings of Christ, so that you may be overjoyed when his glory is revealed" (1 Peter 4:13). To participate in the full life of Christ is to take part in His sufferings as well as His glory. To have the latter without the former would give life a tilted, truncated list.

A tiny nun from Calcutta, India, found this to be true, too. Mother Teresa once said, "We must be able to radiate the joy of Christ, express it in our actions. If our actions are just useful actions that give no joy to people, our poor people would never be able to rise up to the call which we want them to hear, the call to come closer to God. We want them to feel that they are loved. If we went to them with a sad face, we would only make them much more depressed."[2]

Aesop told the fable of two men walking in the woods. One found a hatchet under some brush and said, "Look what I've found." His companion said, "Don't say, 'Look what I've found.' Say, 'Look what we've found.'" A short while later, they came upon a group of men, one of whom claimed that the hatchet was his. The man with the tool said to his friend, "It looks like we're in trouble." The friend responded, "Don't say, 'It looks like we're in trouble.' Say, 'It looks like I'm in trouble.'" Aesop knew that sharing joy and danger went together.

Bill Hybels speaks of joy thus: "Joy—the deep, sustaining joy that Jesus promised—is a gift from God that takes us by surprise. When is it most likely to surprise us? When we are striving, with all our heart and with each passing breath, to live like Jesus did: to lay down our lives freely for others, to live selflessly, without thought for our rewards."[3]

The theme of much of the book of Hebrews is this very thought. The writer addressed people who had recently come to faith in Christ and said, "You sympathized with those in prison and joyfully accepted the confiscation of your property, because you knew that you yourselves had better and lasting possessions" (Heb. 10:34). This same writer told followers of Christ, "Let us fix our eyes on Jesus, the author and perfecter of our faith, who for the joy set before him endured the cross, scorning its shame, and sat down at the right hand of the throne of God" (12:2). Again, this writer referred to those in authority in the church and told Christians, "Obey them so that their work will be a joy, not a burden, for that would be of no advantage" (13:17b).

To live a life of joy does not mean that trouble and pain will never come. It means that joy is a form of energy that helps people live above the circumstances of trouble.

One of the founders of Methodism was John Wesley. On March 29, 1737, he recorded the following words in his journal: "I am convinced as true religion or holiness cannot be without cheerfulness, so steady cheerfulness, on the other hand, cannot be without holiness or true religion. And I am equally convinced that true religion has nothing sour, austere, unsociable, unfriendly in it; but, on the contrary, implies the most winning sweetness, the most amiable softness and gentleness."[4] Wesley lived in the rough and tumble world of circuit riding, but he knew that joy is not dependent on perfect circumstances. It is deep and causes a person to live out a joyful existence. As the Bible puts it, "A cheerful heart is good medicine . . ." (Prov. 17:22). Paul sang in prison. Wesley sang while riding his old horse through a rainstorm in search of a crowd to which to preach. Christians today sing in all sorts of circumstances because of the joy that wells up inside them and effervesces to the surface. This is nothing that can be faked if it is not there, nor is it something that can be checked if it is.

Life is a celebration of being alive. God shares His life with these strange creatures called people. Even with all of the misery in life, how could we not sing for joy? Pioneering heart surgeon Christiaan Barnard once told of making rounds in a children's hospital when he heard some noise. He looked up to see a breakfast trolley that had been commandeered by two kids. One pushed the cart with his head down, and the other, seated on the lower deck, guided the cart by scraping one foot on the floor.

The boy pushing was blind. His parents had gotten drunk one night and fought. The mother threw a lantern at the father. It missed him and broke over the boy's head and shoulders. The flames blinded him and disfigured him for life. The boy who guided the trolley had recently had his arm and shoulder amputated because of bone cancer. Even so, both of the boys put on quite a show for the other kids in the hospital before the "race" ended in scattered plates and a scolding from the nurses. Dr. Barnard wrote about that experience.

> Suddenly, I realized that these two children had given me a profound lesson in getting on with the business of living. Because the business of living is joy in the real sense of the word, not just something for pleasure, amusement, recreation. The business of living is the celebration of being alive. I had been looking at suffering from the wrong end. You don't become a better person because you are suffering; but you become a better person because you have experienced suffering. We can't appreciate light if we haven't known darkness. Nor can we appreciate warmth if we have never suffered cold. These children showed me that it's not what you've lost that's important. What is important is what you have left.[5]

I was interim pastor of a little church in Kentucky for a while several years ago. The first Sunday I went, I saw something I will never forget. A couple in the community attended worship by the only means of transportation they had—a tractor. The man was blind, so he would sit on a seat especially built for him behind the driver's seat. His wife would drive the old machine to church every Sunday, rain or shine.

It's not what you've lost, but what you have left.

I see in my memory a woman plagued for twenty years with obesity, diabetes, cancer, tumors that would build up in her stomach, and other problems. But she knew the inner joy of being alive in Christ, and she lived her faith until she died. I miss her because she was my friend. She taught me something. It's not what you've lost.

How I wish I could remember this truth more clearly, and how I wish I could tell others of it. A man struggling for his life has little time to fuss over whether he is dressed according to the latest fashion guides. I think the refusal of many of us Christians to live in the joy of Christ surely must prompt the tears of God.

I went to the hospital one day to visit two people I had not met. They were friends of people I knew, so I stopped in. The first person poured out a torrent of bitterness, hatred, and envy, even though things were fairly routine with his physical condition, and he had everything going for him financially. When I walked into the next room, I could actually feel the difference of atmosphere. A very old man lay in the bed, and his wife sat by his side. I introduced myself and listened as they told me their story. They had very little in the way of finances when he entered the hospital, and they had even less when I met them. Their mobile home burned while they were in the hospital, and they lost everything they owned. I could have expected the torrent of anger from them that I had heard in the previous room, but it never came. These people were understandably upset and grieving, but they displayed a sense of inner serenity that really stood out. This couple spoke of their faith in Christ, and they lived in the atmosphere of inner joy He provides.

They were living proof for me of what Dr. Barnard and countless others have noticed: it's not what you've lost that counts, but what you have left. What we have left is joy.

Shared Joy

The apostle Paul was away from his beloved friends, the Thessalonians, for a while and felt the tug of loneliness on his heart.

When he wrote to them, he asked, "For what is our hope, our joy, or the crown in which we will glory in the presence of our Lord Jesus when he comes? Is it not you? Indeed, you are our glory and joy" (1 Thess. 2:19–20).

Paul linked his own eternal joy to his friends. Christian joy is social. People are saved as individuals but always are put into a community—the church—to live and work. We are not promised a heaven in which each does his or her own thing, but rather a place where each participates in the life of God. Joy, like life itself, is for sharing.

Paul continued expressing his feelings of this shared experience with the Thessalonians by saying, "For now we really live, since you are standing firm in the Lord. How can we thank God enough for you in return for all the joy we have in the presence of our God because of you?" (1 Thess. 3:8–9). He spoke, too, of the body of Christ as being made of many parts all joined together: "If one part suffers, every part suffers with it; if one part is honored, every part rejoices with it" (1 Cor. 12:26). Paul knew that the lives of God's people—indeed, all people!—are linked inseparably. In a sense, we are all Siamese twins joined at the heart. To separate us is to kill us. As a friend of mine is used to saying, "Well, we'll have to hang together, or we'll all hang separately."

I once attended a meeting of deaf Christians to write a story for a religious news service. While there, I met a young man named Scott. He had been born both deaf and blind. But Scott radiated joy like a steam radiator gives off heat. The smile on his face was something to see. An interpreter helped me talk to Scott. He held the interpreter's hands while she signed to him my questions and statements. Then he let go and signed back the answers, and the interpreter relayed the information to me. At first I thought it would be a clumsy way to communicate, but Scott was communicating much to me. He was alive in Christ and had joy in his heart. It showed all over. He said through the interpreter, "God has spoken to me here! Christians, Christians, here!" Yes, joy is for sharing, and Scott shared it easily.

Pearl Bailey, that energetic actress of *Hello, Dolly!* fame, once said that her husband told her she worries about people too much. Pearl replied, "I don't worry; I care." Exactly! She cares. And people in Christ are called to a life of caring that shares both the pain and the joys of others. This is what helps us live out our lives, lonely though they might be. In a deep sense, we never fully escape the loneliness that seems to surround us like a shroud, and we do not need to escape it. A thoughtful writer reflected on this condition:

> The Christian way of life does not take away our loneliness; it protects and cherishes it as a precious gift. Sometimes it seems as if we do everything possible to avoid the painful confrontation with our basic human loneliness, and allow ourselves to be trapped by false gods promising immediate satisfaction and quick relief. But perhaps the painful awareness of loneliness is an invitation to transcend our limitations and look beyond the boundaries of our existence. The awareness of loneliness might be a gift we must protect and guard, because our loneliness reveals to us an inner emptiness that can be destructive when misunderstood, but filled with promise for him who can tolerate its sweet pain.[6]

Joy is part of the fruit of the Spirit. It is shared and helps intensify and transfigure every area of life, even loneliness.

Consider how this happens in your own life. You open the mail and find a card from a friend who has remembered your birthday. You answer the phone and hear the familiar voice of an old acquaintance who is calling just to see how things are going. You open the door and find someone on the steps whom you have not seen in a while and whom you have been missing. Joy comes in living, and especially in sharing time with someone about whom we care. It comes, too, from reaching out and sharing ourselves with others. After all, you are really the only gift you have to give away. Be glad! Rejoice! God had given you life, and time, and the gift of joy. As Francis of Assisi put it, "Let us leave sadness to the devil and his angels. As for us, what can we be but rejoicing and glad?"

Finding Joy

Where is joy to be found? If it is a fruit of the Spirit, on what vine does it grow? In whose garden? At the hand of what farmer? People of God through the ages have known that joy comes by knowing the Giver of joy. The psalmist wrote,

> When the LORD brought back the captives to Zion,
>   we were like men who dreamed.
>   Our mouths were filled with laughter,
>   our tongues with songs of joy.
>   Then it was said among the nations,
>   "The LORD has done great things for them."
>   The LORD has done great things for us,
>   and we are filled with joy. (Ps. 126:1–3)

God gives such joy as men and women hunger after Him. Again, the psalmist says:

> O God, you are my God,
>   earnestly I seek you;
>   my soul thirsts for you,
>   my body longs for you,
>   in a dry and weary land
>   where there is no water. . . .
>   My soul will be satisfied as with the richest
>   of foods; with singing lips my mouth will
>   praise you. (Ps. 63:1, 5)

God gives the gift of joy to people who seek Him rather than to those who seek joy. This is partially because joy is gained on the slant rather than by a frontal assault. Have you ever had trouble going to sleep? If you lie in bed thinking "I will go to sleep! I will go to sleep!" you will probably wake up even more. You do not work at going to sleep. Instead, you relax and let it come. Finding joy is like this, too.

When we seek God, we find Him and His gifts. In finding God, we are changed, and our thinking and our seeing are transformed.

We find joy—or maybe I should say that joy finds us—as we look at life through God's eyes. This is never possible in an absolute sense, but it is in an approximate sense. When I do this, I take myself out of the focus in the center of the picture. Someone else is there, and once I have gotten outside my own little world, I discover the joy of the rest of God's creation. Eugene Peterson says, "Joy is the capacity to hear the name [of God] and to recognize that God is here. There's a kind of exhilaration because God is doing something and, even in a little way, it's enough at the moment."[7] W. R. Inge wrote about this experience thus:

> Joy will be ours insofar as we are genuinely interested in great ideas outside ourselves. When we have once crossed the charmed circle and got outside ourselves, we shall soon realize that all true joy has an eternal and Divine source and goal. We are immortal spirits, set to do certain things in time; were it not so, our lives would lack any rational justification. The joy of achievement is the recognition of a task understood and done. It is done, and fit to take its place—however lowly a place—in the eternal order. . . . To do our duty in our own sphere, to try to create something worth creating, as our life's work, is the way to understand what joy is in this life, and by God's grace to earn the verdict: "Well done, good and faithful servant; enter thou into the joy of thy Lord."[8]

Someone who cannot get outside his or her own skin can never find joy. People like this are too wrapped up in their own tiny universes to be concerned about others or about God.

Many people remember when the space shuttle *Challenger* tragically exploded in January 1986. The major television networks carried the coverage live that day. Local stations reported being swamped by angry callers who did not want their soap operas interrupted for any reason. A secretary at one station tried to explain the tragedy and said some people responded, "Yes, it is a tragedy all right. I can't watch *As the World Turns*." How could such a person ever hope to know something as other-centered as joy?

The late L. D. Johnson said of Jesus that His "happiness corresponded to the universal law that joy comes from self-forgetfulness. The happiest people are the very people who are most interested in other people and are doing most for them. The surest recipe for a joyless, meaningless life is to look at yourself constantly and interpret all reality in terms of how it affects you."[9] How I wish this message could be given to the viewers of television dramas.

Fortunately, many people through the ages have realized what Johnson tried to communicate. One such person, W. B. Wolfe, reflected on happiness and realized that joy cannot be chased down like a dollar bill blowing in the wind. He said, "If you observe a really happy man, you will find him building a boat, writing a symphony, educating his son, growing double dahlias in his garden, or looking for dinosaur eggs in the Gobi Desert. He will not be searching for happiness as if it were a collar button that has rolled under the radiator. He will not be striving for it as a goal in itself."[10]

Joy comes to us when we are found by God and when we give our lives to Him. Everything in life then becomes a conduit of grace.

In his book titled simply *Joy,* Louis Evely took seriously the promise of John 16:20b: "You will grieve, but your grief will turn to joy." Evely wrote, "When you have become penetrated with the joy of God, all of your sorrows will turn into joy, all of your trials will be graces; you will recognize your faults, you will be sorry for them, and they will be forgiven so that they may become happy faults. They will remind you only of the goodness, the tenderness, the joy with which God forgives them."[11]

Think of the truly joy-filled people you know. Are they not the ones who are always willing to help others and get involved with them? Are they not the ones who spend little or no time complaining about how they feel or that no one calls them or that life has passed them by? God wants this for all His children.

The fruit of the Spirit is joy. Why not pick some for yourself as you learn to live for others?

Peace is liberty in tranquillity.

—Cicero

Chapter 3

The Elusive Butterfly
P E A C E

A JEWISH FRIEND OF MINE who grew up in Tel Aviv, Israel, once gave me a gift from his native country—a menorah, the seven-candle holder that is the ancient symbol of peace. Across the front of it is printed the word *shalom,* the Hebrew word for peace. Although I have not seen my friend for a long time, his gift is dear to me. It reminds me of our college days together. He was discovering America, struggling with English, and trying to make sense of Christianity. So was I! This same friend gave me his Israeli "G.I." copy of his Bible—an Old Testament written in Hebrew.

A menorah and a Bible. These are powerful reminders to me of what Paul called part of the fruit of the Spirit—peace. Peace is like a gentle butterfly that we spend our lives chasing but seldom seem to catch. But we must continue the struggle to gain it. As Paul put it, "Let the peace of Christ rule in your hearts" (Col. 3:15a). The strange thing about it, though, is that while we are to be peacemakers, we cannot go out and order a day's supply of peace the way we might lay in a supply of firewood. Peace is a gift of God. It cannot be netted, but it can be accepted.

Consider, for example, the following two people. One spent much of his life grabbing after peace for his own purposes. The other sought not peace as an end in itself but the God who gives peace.

Seeking Peace for Its Own Sake

The autopsy listed his name as Louis Hubert Casebolt, but for years he was known to his followers as "Archanna Christos," which means the "oldest anointed one."[1] This man had been a spiritual teacher, a former convict, soldier, evangelist, and father of a communal family related by the quest for inner peace. His thirty-year search for inner peace ended when he placed a .22-caliber rifle under his chin and pulled the trigger. His "family" members were people who had given up their former lives to share Casebolt's vision. He gave up much, such as most material things and modern tools, in the search for what he called the "intuitive consciousness." The followers of this man lived together in a marsh commune known as VelaAshby in Plaquemines Parish in Louisiana. The goal was to live off the land and find inner peace through communing with nature.

Casebolt had lived an unusual life. He had gone to prison for manslaughter as a teenager. After his release, he served as a gunner on a B-17 bomber and was wounded in action during the war. Later he was an evangelist, pulling in some five hundred dollars per week in the 1950s. He gave that up because he felt that the thinking of most people was unoriginal and that they were too easily guided by the rigidity of organized religion to trouble themselves about inner meaning and peace.

This man's life was tragic on several levels. He began seeking the God of peace but gave up this search to go his own way and find peace of mind on his own terms. Furthermore, he lead others with him to a commune in an escape from "ordinary" living. He also took his life in what appears to be a last attempt to find peace, if not in this life then perhaps in the next.

I respond to this man's life in several ways. For one thing, I am sympathetic to his search, but I think he went about it in the wrong way. Further, I agree with his opinion that too many people simply believe what anyone tells them in the area of religion and do not bother to search out the truth on their own. Mostly, though, I feel compassion for a man who had a rough time in life and who was never quite able to "put it together." Peace is such an elusive state of mind. It certainly eluded Louis Casebolt.

Even Christians can get caught up in this dead-ended grapple for peace for its own sake. Some of contemporary Christianity tends to take basic religious beliefs and practices and turn them into various expressions of selfishness. Some people say they read the Bible because it makes them feel good. Reading the Bible certainly can make them feel good, but that is not the primary reason for digging into the Scriptures. Some churches encourage people to tithe to get more from God. That might happen, but stewardship is not a lottery. Some of the most popular religious books emphasize prepackaged ways of making Christianity "work" and gaining personal gratification. Lynn Clayton says of this trend, "Don't look for best sellers entitled *Humility—God's Way* or *Serving Others Before Self*. Look for books entitled *God's Way to Financial Abundance* and *How I Prayed Myself Thin*. The way to write a best-selling religious book is to take culture's runaway self-centeredness, wrap it with a thin coat of religious sweetness and give it a catchy title."[2]

What is the answer for such a perversion? Clayton answers,

> We must let the Bible speak in its entirety. We must hear the Scriptures proclaim that we find our lives by losing them, and that we are to take up our crosses—and believe that they mean just that. We must stop trying to shape the Bible into some kind of formula for personal success presentation based on religiousized positive thinking. The church must be secure enough in its faith to realize the gospel will not be popular among all people and that the lowly Galilean was more interested in people's total well-being than just their financial success. The church must emulate the humble spirit and attitude of the Carpenter in all we do.

We can so easily get lulled into thinking that peace is an object or an attitude that can be our private possession if we just search for it enough. We might imagine that to be at peace means that we will have no trouble or pain or sorrow. But Jesus was the Prince of Peace, and he got nailed to a cross! There certainly is peace to be found even in this strife-wracked world. As Proverbs 14:30 puts it, "Peace of mind makes the body healthy, but jealousy is like a cancer" (TEV). What I am trying to say is that peace comes primarily as a by-product of searching for God and not primarily by searching for peace itself.

Some of the Christians in Germany during the Second World War learned this lesson in a painful way. One pastor, Martin Niemöller, spoke after the war about what happened when people were concerned only with their own peace. Niemöller said, "In Germany they came first for the Communists; I did not speak out because I was not a Communist. Then they came for the Jews; I did not speak because I was not a Jew. Then they came to fetch the workers, members of the trade unions; I did not speak because I was not a trade unionist. Afterward, they came for the Catholics; I did not say anything because I was a Protestant. Eventually they came for me, and there was no one left to speak."

I saw a cartoon once in which a man walked into a bookstore. He saw displayed on the shelves books with titles such as *How to Think Right, How to Be Happy, Positive Thinking, The Easy Way, Don't Worry,* and *Mind at Rest.* The customer said to the owner, "Have you got something that won't give me cow-like complacency about the world? I want to be concerned, stimulated, stirred, worried. . . ." Closing yourself off from the pain of the rest of the world is no sure way to find peace. In fact, it is the sure way *not* to find it.

Searching for the God of Peace

Now I want you to consider another man who found peace in a completely different way from Casebolt, the man mentioned earlier. Instead of searching for peace as a quality or a possession in itself, this man first sought God, for God gives peace as a blessing to those who follow Him. The man to whom I am referring is St. Francis of Assisi, who lived from 1181 to 1226.

Francis was a man of prayer and peaceful actions. When prayer and peaceful actions are linked together, powerful things happen, both within the person who brings them together and in the world around such a person. Francis was convinced that the God of peace should be known by all persons, regardless of their position or background. In the thirteenth century, the church was involved in what it called the Fifth Crusade. Followers of Muhammad had captured the Holy Land, and the church was spending so much time and energy hating and fighting these men that it had quite forgotten that the real work of the church is to witness to God's love. The church wanted to force the Moslems to become Christians by defeating them in battle. But what kind of a profession could come at a knife's point? Francis asked, "What is the use of trying to conquer the Sultan? We must win him by love instead."

In the summer of 1219, Francis sailed with a little band of companions dedicated to preaching the gospel to the Moslems. They landed in Egypt and joined the army of the Crusaders. Francis and one of his companions left the lines of the Crusaders and made their way toward the camp of the Saracens. They knew they were risking their lives in doing so, yet they were as calm as if they were walking the open road in Assisi. As they walked, they sang the words of the Twenty-third Psalm: "The Lord is my shepherd; I shall not want. . . . Yea, though I walk through the valley of the shadow of death, I will fear no evil: for thou art with me."

Francis and his companion were seized and bound by Arabs who dragged them before one officer after another. To each Francis made the same calm reply: "I am a Christian, take me to your lord." At last, they were taken to the Sultan himself. He asked them who they were and from where they had come. Francis answered, "We have been sent not by man but by God to tell you and your people of the love of Christ." Then Francis preached the gospel of Christ's love.

The Sultan listened with respect and surprise to what Francis had to say. He was impressed by the courage and enthusiasm of the missionary who had risked his life to enter an enemy camp. The Sultan asked the two Christians to stay with him, and Francis answered, "If you or your people will become followers of Christ, for His love I will willingly remain with you." While the men in the Saracens camp held Francis in great honor because of his courage, they were not prepared to become followers of Christ. Francis thought that staying there would then be useless. The Sultan allowed him to return to the Christian camp. The Sultan's parting words to Francis were, "Pray for me that God may show me that law and faith which are according to His own heart."[3]

Because of his bold actions in Christ's name, and because of his burning desire to serve God regardless of the cost, Francis found the peace for which so many people search. And because peace was an inner reality for him, he could write the prayer that is now so well known:

> Lord,
> Make me an instrument of Thy peace.
> Where there is hatred, let me sow love;
> Where there is injury, pardon;
> Where there is doubt, faith;
> Where there is despair, hope;
> Where there is darkness, light;
> Where there is sadness, joy.
> O, Divine Master,
> Grant that I may not so much
> Seek to be consoled, as to console;
> To be understood, as to understand;
> To be loved, as to love.
> For it is in giving that we receive,
> It is in pardoning that we are pardoned,
> And it is in dying, that we are born to eternal life.

Francis surely understood Jesus' teaching when He said, "Have salt in yourselves, and be at peace with each other" (Mark 9:50b). Salt is both a preserving and a seasoning agent. Peace, like salt, preserves and seasons life. Francis understood this fact. Why else would he have risked his life to go into the enemy camp to carry the gospel? His selflessness is precisely what could bring about the possibilities of peace.

Solomon, too, knew how to pursue peace. First Kings 3 tells how God told him to ask for whatever he wanted most. Most people probably would have asked for riches, fame, and long life. But Solomon responded thus: "Now, O LORD my God, you have made your servant king in place of my father David. But I am only a little child and do not know how to carry out my duties. Your servant is here among the people you have chosen, a great people, too numerous to count or number. So give your servant a discerning heart to govern your people and to distinguish between right and wrong. For who is able to govern this great people of yours?" (1 Kings 3:7–9).

How did God respond? "So God said to him, 'Since you have asked for this and not for long life or wealth for yourself, nor have asked for the death of your enemies but for discernment in administering justice, I will do what you have asked. I will give you a wise and discerning heart, so that there will never have been anyone like you, nor will there ever be'" (1 Kings 3:11–12).

Solomon got what he requested, plus more besides, but the point is that he did not ask for things that would enrich himself. His request was for the ability to help his people. No wonder his life was peaceful in the ultimate sense.

Solomon's request reminds me of the prayer written by some unknown Confederate soldier. Perhaps you have seen this:

> I asked God for strength, that I might achieve;
> I was made weak, that I might learn humbly to obey.
> I asked for health, that I might do greater things;
> I was given infirmity that I might do better things.
> I asked for riches, that I might be happy;
> I was given poverty, that I might be wise.
> I asked for power, that I might have the praise of men;
> I was given weakness, that I might feel the need of God.
> I asked for all things, that I might enjoy life;
> I was given life that I might enjoy all things.
> I got nothing that I asked for—but everything I had hoped for.
> Almost despite myself, my unspoken prayers were answered.
> I am among men, most richly blessed.

The man or woman who can learn to lean on God and trust in His purposes in life can learn to receive peace. This is why the psalmist could write so movingly in Psalm 91:

> He who dwells in the shelter of the Most High
>> will rest in the shadow of the Almighty.
> I will say of the LORD, "He is my refuge and my fortress,
>> my God, in whom I trust."
> Surely he will save you from the fowler's snare
>> and from the deadly pestilence.
> He will cover you with his feathers,
>> and under his wings you will find refuge;
>> his faithfulness will be your shield and rampart.
> You will not fear the terror of night,
>> nor the arrow that flies by day,
> nor the pestilence that stalks in the darkness,
>> nor the plague that destroys at midday.
> A thousand may fall at your side,
>> ten thousand at your right hand,
>> but it will not come near you. (vv. 1–7)

How well we would sleep if we could pray such a prayer each evening!

Finding the Peace of God

Peace, that elusive butterfly, seems always ready to flap its wings and swish out of reach. You grab for it, but it eludes your reach. But do not give up in despair. Instead, allow it to come to you. The peace that God gives is the deepest and most satisfying we may know. There are several things we can do to get it. Let me suggest a few.

The first thing is to learn to seek and cultivate silence sometimes. For whatever reason, God does not like to shout over the roar of our lives. Yet how noisy our lives are. We can hardly seem to get away from these noises. I remember when our twin sons, Chris and Ryan, were little. They were normal, healthy boys in constant overdrive. Finding times of quiet around our house was difficult, but finding it was even more essential because of the usual chaos. There were times when I simply needed to still the external and internal noises so I could listen for God. I still need that today.

Think of the noises in your life that quell peace. The alarm clock buzzes the blissful dreams out of your head the first thing in the morning. The children get up grumpy. Your spouse is not little Miss (or Mr.) Sunshine. You pour the wrong cereal for one kid, and the other one cannot find his shoes. You are late for work, and voices rise in direct proportion to the number of minutes you are behind schedule. Traffic is crazy and congested on your way, and the office or factory or school is no better. People pull at you all day, the phone never seems to stop ringing, and one hassle after another seems to have your name on it. When quitting time comes, you are worn to the proverbial frazzle. You would like nothing better than to lie back in your favorite chair for an hour and regroup the internal forces. But there is traffic to fight, kids to pick up, the PTA meeting, the choir practice, the car that needs realigning, the dishes that need washing, the beds that need changing, and on and on it goes. How can you find silence in a life like that?

Such a pace makes finding some quiet even more important. Getting up a little earlier or going to bed a little later is one way of finding a few extra minutes. Learning to use travel time for prayer and Bible listening is helpful. Invest in a copy of the New Testament on cassette and listen to it, if possible, while you travel. The Bible was originally transmitted by word of mouth before everyone had written copies. Listening to it lends a different dimension from reading it. If you are married, perhaps rearranging the household schedule and duties can free up a little time for personal reflection and quietness.

Psalm 131 has only three verses, but they are powerful:

> My heart is not proud, O Lord,
>   my eyes are not haughty;
> I do not concern myself with great matters
>   or things too wonderful for me.

> *But I have stilled and quieted my soul;*
>   like a weaned child with its mother,
>   like a weaned child is my soul within me.
> O Israel, put your hope in the LORD
>   both now and forevermore. (Italics added)

"I have stilled and quieted my soul." Those words cut right through me because they remind me how vital this is to my whole well-being. Even Jesus found that He had to withdraw to quiet places for times of reflection and prayer. If *He* needed it, what about *us?*

Some of you reading these words have the opposite problem from what I am describing. For you, life is already quiet—too quiet. You might be single or widowed. You would give anything for some excitement, some tension, some noise. A married friend, who because of physical problems can never have a child, was visiting in our home one day. My wife and I were apologizing for the noisiness of our boys, and I said, "There are times I would give anything for an hour of silence." This friend looked at me and said, "And there are times when I would give anything for an hour of laughing children."

Many people are living lives that are too quiet and seem at times devoid of some of the richness that life has to offer. To them—to you reading this, if you are such a person—I say that that condition can give you special access to the deep things of the Spirit that the rest of us may not know. The slower pace and less distracted nature of your circumstances can allow you to commune with the God of peace. You may know an inner peace that is beyond what many people who seem to have everything will ever know. As Paul once put it, "I have learned the secret of being content in any and every situation . . ." (Phil. 4:12b).

Ann Morrow Lindbergh wrote about this sense of seeking peace. She noted, "But I want first of all . . . to be at peace with myself. I want a singleness of eye, a purity of intention, a central core to my life. . . . I want, in fact—to borrow from the language of the saints— to live 'in grace' as much of the time as possible."[4] Lindbergh pointed out that by "grace" she meant "inner harmony, essentially spiritual, which can be translated into outward harmony." She discovered what millions of people during the last two millennia have known: peace comes to us inwardly through the gift of God and then works its way outwardly as peaceable acts toward others.

Another way to gain the peace of God is to avoid those things that war against peace, and seek those things that lead to it. All of us, no matter how strong we might be, are influenced by our surroundings and other people. A child who grows up in a home where chaos and anger reign begins with two strikes against him. A young person whose friends are evil-minded troublemakers has a very tough time breaking free of such an influence to live for Christ. A person who works with associates who think that life is nothing but *bon temp roulette*—let the good times roll—will have to work doubly hard to find the peace that Paul describes as part of the fruit of the Spirit.

This problem has always existed. Consider the dilemma of the man described in Psalm 120:5–6:

> Woe to me that I dwell in Meshech,
>   that I live among the tents of Kedar!
> Too long have I lived
>   among those who hate peace.
> I am a man of peace;
>   but when I speak, they are for war.

I know how he felt. I, too, "live among the tents of Kedar," among those who are aggressive and pugnacious. I, too, live among those who are always talking about showing someone—whether it be an individual or another nation—how "tough" they are. Unfortunately, this is not all just talk but is action, too. Men, women, and children of peace cry out to God that we might regain some sense of fairness and equality about us. Jesus came as the "Prince of Peace." It is not that He gave in and backed off from every challenge. In fact, He faced each one. He challenged the warmongers by being a tough-minded peacemaker. He calls His followers to be people of peace, even if it costs them everything. How difficult this is!

An expert on violent behavior has noted that media violence is programming America's children to kill.[5] Children who take guns to school to massacre classmates learn that behavior. Dave Grossman says that some of the techniques the military uses to teach soldiers to kill are now being used by media in the guise of entertainment. They include desensitization, brutalization, classical conditioning, operant conditioning, and role modeling. He contends, "Our children watch vivid pictures of human suffering and death, and they learn to associate it with their favorite soft drink and candy bar, or their girlfriend's perfume."

This is a frightening picture of life today. That is why we need to swim against the current, to struggle to live and model a different way of doing things. A lady recently died in a nearby community. She had lived as a follower of the "Prince of Peace." Her beliefs were tested one day. While minding her own business several years ago, life suddenly turned upside down. An escaped convict walked into her house and pointed a shotgun at her. She said to him, "You sit down here. I don't want no violence. I am a Christian lady, and I want you to put that gun down." He did! She prepared breakfast for him and taught him to pray over his meal. He didn't know what to say, so she told him to say, "Jesus wept." He did. After the meal, she talked him into giving himself up. But life was different when he went back to prison. The convict and his former hostage kept in touch. She taught him how to live. He said of her, "She's not just one of those people who run around saying they're Christians. The way she reacted to me, her faith was so strong that she acted like a Christian."[6]

Peace, to be lived, must be cultivated as a delicate flower. Tender care, constant attention, and, if necessary, drastic action are sometimes required. But this is difficult. It takes a lifelong commitment. Someone wrote about this matter thus: "All too often, we Christians seek 'peace'—the sticky unloving kind that has as its goal only our own freedom from discomfort or danger. Our Lord is the Prince of Peace, who always seeks the true peace even at the cost of disturbing the peace. And today he asks the same of all who aspire to be his followers."[7]

Near the old provincial capital of Ou Dong, Cambodia, the countryside is littered with empty bullet shells. These are the leftovers of a civil war that ravaged the country many years ago. Children find these spent shells and take them to local foundries where they are melted down and recast as bells to be hung on the necks of oxen. Where once the brass was the casings for shells and destruction, it is now the means of the gentle ringing of bells as the Cambodians go about their work.[8]

From shells to bells—this is the hope of all who follow the master of peace. It is the "swords to plowshares" dream of Isaiah, and the "Day of the Lord" hope of Joel. But how does this hope become reality for Christians today? It comes through our participation in the cross of Christ. Paul said it this way: "May I never boast except in the cross of our Lord Jesus Christ, through which the world has been crucified to me, and I to the world. Neither circumcision nor uncircumcision means anything; what counts is a new creation. Peace and mercy to all who follow this rule, even to the Israel of God" (Gal. 6:14–16).

Paul promised the peace of God to those who participate in the life of Christ by being crucified to the world and it to them. This does not mean literal death, but rather the putting to death those attitudes and actions that ruin the prospects of living God's reality. In other words, I cannot pray and hope for peace if I am unwilling to get out of the rat race of competition and self-promotion. Peace will indeed be the "elusive butterfly" until I am remolded into the likeness of Christ (see Phil. 2:5–11). Even then, Christ's peace will be vastly different from simple freedom from discomfort or annoyance. That is not peace anyway—it is boredom!

Many years ago, a document was written that has become known as the *Desiderata*. It exudes the sort of wisdom that can lead to peace. Consider its counsel:

> Go placidly amid the noise and haste, and remember what peace there may be in silence. As far as possible without surrender be on good terms with all persons. Speak your truth quietly and clearly; and listen to others, even the dull and ignorant; they too have their story.
>
> Avoid loud and aggressive persons; they are vexations to the spirit. If you compare yourself with others, you may

become vain and bitter; for always there will be greater and lesser persons than yourself. Enjoy your achievements as well as your plans.

Keep interested in your own career, however humble; it is a real possession in the changing fortunes of time. Exercise caution in your business affairs; for the world is full of trickery. But let this not blind you to what virtue there is; many persons strive for high ideals; and everywhere life is full of heroism.

Be yourself. Especially, do not feign affection. Neither be cynical about love; for in the face of all aridity and disenchantment it is as perennial as the grass.

Take kindly the counsel of the years, gracefully surrendering the things of youth. Nurture strength of spirit to shield you in sudden misfortune. But do not distress yourself with imaginings. Many fears are born of fatigue and loneliness. Beyond a wholesome discipline be gentle with yourself.

You are a child of the universe, no less than the trees and the stars; you have a right to be here. And whether or not it is clear to you, no doubt the universe is unfolding as it should.

Therefore be at peace with God, whatever you conceive Him to be; and whatever your labors and aspirations, in the noisy confusion of life keep peace with your soul.

With all its sham, drudgery, and broken dreams, it is still a beautiful world. Be careful. Strive to be happy.

I would argue with some of the sentiment of this document, but on the whole I find it helpful to me as I try to pick part of the fruit of the Spirit—peace. Truly this is a virtue of grace that cannot be captured by force, but it can be lured by love. What are you using for bait?

Genius . . . is only long patience. Work.
      —Gustave Flaubert

Chapter 4

Hang On and Hold Out
PATIENCE

To get what you want in life, you first must know what you want—and then have the drive to make those dreams come true. Having an active imagination and boundless energy is not enough. You must also have patience.[1]

So says Dr. Martin Groder, a psychiatrist and business consultant. He calls patience "strategic waiting." It is the ability to wait actively, to think and plan, and not to jump to hasty conclusions before getting the facts. Whether in business or other important areas of life, patience is necessary because not everything we want can be had now.

Think of the ways life can get complicated and frustrating. How, for example, does the mother of a physically handicapped child keep going and refuse to give up? How does a man with a bad job find the strength to go to work every day to earn a paycheck instead of quitting and letting his family go hungry? How do people living in poverty find the inner courage to keep struggling to do the best they can? *Patience.*

Patience, in the biblical sense, is not sitting idly by while the world goes on. It is not even wishful thinking. Patience, as part of the fruit of the Spirit, is the deep, personal knowledge that God is working in your life and in His world. This knowledge allows the mother of a handicapped child to keep working and doing the best she can. It helps the man with a not-so-great job to go on with the job without investing all of his hopes and dreams in the business. Patience has been defined as "living out the belief that God orders everything for the spiritual good of his children. Patience does not just grin and bear things, stoic-like, but accepts them cheerfully as therapeutic workouts planned by a heavenly trainer who is resolved to get you up to full fitness."[2]

But this is obviously easier said than done! It is one thing to accept such a definition mentally but another thing altogether to accept it emotionally. We do not live out of definitions but out of that complex interrelation of mind, body, and spirit. Our bodies, for example, might seem to be in open revolt against us, but still the mind and spirit can overcome all resistance and end up serving a loving heavenly Father. This takes patience, which is active participation in the will of God, and not just passive waiting. A well-known writer put it this way: "The Christian patience is not a grim, bleak acceptance of a situation; even the patience is irradiated with joy. *The Christian waits, not as one who waits for the night, but as one who waits for the morning.*"[3]

I am reminded of a line from one of the comic operas of Gilbert and Sullivan: "Do you know what it is to seek oceans and find puddles?"

I answer that question, "Yes! I do." I guess that you do, too. We want so much. We want good things, even great things, not in the sense of possessions, but quality of life and mind. But we find that we cannot have everything we desire. Life seems rather fizzled out at times, and each day seems a carbon copy of the one before it. How do we deal with the puddles when we are taught to seek oceans? The answer is through that strength of inner life that the Bible calls patience. This come from a God who is patient.

The Patience of God

Older versions of the Bible call patience *long-suffering*. That is a highly descriptive term that is used even of God. I sometimes wonder what life would be like if God were like me—or anyone else, for that matter. How would He relate to the world? If God were like me, He would have tired of the whole swampy mess a long time ago and would have destroyed it. Thank heavens that God is not like me or you.

The prophet Jeremiah gives us a picture of God's patience. Jeremiah went to a potter's house and watched him working at his wheel shaping pottery. "But the pot he was shaping from the clay was marred in his hands; so the potter formed it into another pot, shaping it as seemed best to him. Then the word of the Lord came to me: 'O house of Israel, can I not do with you as this potter does?' declares the Lord. 'Like clay in the hand of the potter, so are you in my hand, O house of Israel'" (Jer. 18:4–6).

This is a powerful image. It tells us that God has in mind a design and a goal for people. God keeps moving people toward this goal and design. He is the patient Potter who shapes and forms and molds the clay. Even when it gets marred in His hand He does not simply throw it away, but He reshapes it.

The Old Testament affirms the patience of God toward people. Exodus 34:6–7a states, "And he [God] passed in front of Moses, proclaiming, 'The Lord, the Lord, the compassionate and gracious God, slow to anger, abounding in love and faithfulness, maintaining love to thousands, and forgiving wickedness, rebellion and sin.'" The second half of verse 7 puts this patience in perspective, however: "Yet he does not leave the guilty unpunished. . . ." God is no tottering, senile, grandfatherly being who sits in His heavenly rocking chair, allowing people to do whatever they wish! He is "slow to anger" because He wants people to change, and God knows that change is not easy.

Nehemiah referred to his spiritual ancestors in Israel and said in a prayer to the Lord, "But you are a forgiving God, gracious and compassionate, slow to anger and abounding in love. Therefore you did not desert them . . ." (Neh. 9:17b). The Psalms echo this assessment about God. Psalm 86:15 sounds nearly like

Nehemiah: "But you, O Lord, are a compassionate and gracious God, slow to anger, abounding in love and faithfulness." Psalm 103:8 says, "The Lord is compassionate and gracious, slow to anger, abounding in love." Psalm 145:8 puts it this way: "The Lord is gracious and compassionate, slow to anger and rich in love."

This sounds like good news, but at least one person in the Old Testament did not like God's patience. Jonah went as a reluctant missionary to Nineveh to preach repentance, and to his great surprise—and regret!—the people repented. God was good to His promise not to destroy them, and Jonah did not like that one bit. Chapter 4 of Jonah begins thus: "But Jonah was greatly displeased and became angry. He prayed to the Lord, 'O Lord, is this not what I said when I was still at home? That is why I was so quick to flee to Tarshish. I knew that you are a gracious and compassionate God, slow to anger and abounding in love, a God who relents from sending calamity. Now, O Lord, take away my life, for it is better for me to die than to live'" (v. 1–3).

To this whining of Jonah, God asks one question: "Have you any right to be angry?" (v. 4). The implied answer was, of course, no.

The New Testament states even more clearly that God is patient with His strange creation called human beings. Paul spoke of himself as the worst of sinners, a blasphemer, and a persecutor. But God was patient with him to save him. "But for that very reason I was shown mercy so that in me, the worst of sinners, Christ Jesus might display his unlimited patience as an example for those who would believe on him and receive eternal life" (1 Tim. 1:16). Peter also affirmed the patience of God that leads to salvation: "The Lord is not slow in keeping his promise, as some understand slowness. He is patient with you, not wanting anyone to perish, but everyone to come to repentance" (2 Peter 3:9). Peter also said of this, "Bear in mind that our Lord's patience means salvation, just as our dear brother Paul also wrote you with the wisdom that God gave him" (2 Peter 3:15).

God waits with a holy patience for people to come to their senses and give their lives to Him. He waits for people to come alive to the possibilities of living in union with Him. He waits as people wear out many a hammer against the anvil of His patience and finally realize that they are His, no matter what. God waits on us.

And we wait on God. I do not mean anything sacrilegious with this statement. What I do mean is that patience is required on our part as we work to understand God more fully and to live in that understanding. Do you know everything about God? Do you fully understand His ways? Of course not! And neither does anyone else. I often wonder about God's way in the world. I cannot comprehend it fully, so I must live with an assurance that it is all combining and interacting for the good of those who love Him (see Rom. 8:28). God does things that I might not do if the choice were mine. But, thank goodness, God does not need my permission to do what He knows is the best.

Life is challenging and often puzzling. We do not know why some people seem to have ten talents while others have only one or two. We need patience to live with the realization that God does not consult with us before giving His gifts. One of the great mysteries is that God's best gift, His Son, was born in a stable with its numbing cold and the smell of cattle dung. How unmatched were the gift and the container! God gives all things to those who live in Him and wait. As Paul put it, "If God is for us, who can be against us? He who did not spare his own Son, but gave him up for us all—how will he not also, along with him, graciously give us all things?" (Rom. 8:31–32).

Cultivating the Art of Patient Living

Patience is the God-given power of creative waiting. This is far different from twiddling your thumbs while resting in your favorite recliner and hoping that things get better. The Spirit of God gives patience as part of His fruit. Therefore, it is to be cultivated, tended, cared for, valued, and protected.

Waiting is one thing, but creative waiting is quite another. This is the very hard task of life navigation. You want to do something—make a career change, for example—but find that you cannot do it now. Several possibilities are open to you. For one thing, you could sit around and bemoan the job you have now and berate everyone associated with it. But all this will do is make you more miserable and hurt you by making you continually angry. Another option is to tell the boss off and quit tomorrow. But the bills will still show up in the mailbox with frightening regularity, so this will not do. A third possibility is to focus your energy and attention in another direction to things that interest you. For example, a secretary who is bored with her job might spend her off-duty time studying to become a real estate agent. This is creative waiting. It is being willing to do one thing for a while—in this example, staying with the secretarial job—until something better can be entered, namely, the real estate sales position.

Parents of small children learn this kind of patience. They are willing to put up with cereal on the ceiling and marbles in the bathtub drain because they know that something better will come.

Patience is the power to get out of our relationships all that is possible. I do not know everything about God, but I act on what I do know as I try to be patient to understand more. This is also true of work, marriage, friendship, parenthood, and spiritual life.

Take, for example, the matter of work. We will spend about one hundred thousand hours of our lives working. Do we enjoy it and feel fulfilled by our job? Or do we feel drained, depleted, and deadened? Biblical patience gives us the ability to create our paths in life rather than just jumping at anything that comes along.

Bill Galston once took a job as Deputy Assistant to the President of the United States for Domestic Policy. The job was challenging, exciting, and demanding. While Galston found the job enjoyable, he also found that it took him away from what he loved best—his family. His nine-year-old son, Ezra, enjoyed baseball but realized that his father could not be there to watch him play. Ezra wrote his father a letter in which he said, "Baseball's not fun when there's no one there to applaud you." Galston knew what he had to do. He resigned his high-profile job and got his life back in balance. He said of that experience, "It wasn't as if I were giving up something I didn't care about. But I was giving it up in favor of something I cared about even more. Fatherhood is the prism through which I see the world. Nothing else is even a close second."[4] This wise man had the patience to struggle through the complexities of life until he could find what he knew was the right path for himself and his family.

Did you know that a patient, thoughtful approach to life can also help you live longer? A study by the Harvard Medical School confirmed that being a "grumpy old man" increases by three times the likelihood of death from heart disease. The seven-year study followed 1,305 men ages forty to ninety. They were categorized in terms of their ability or inability to control anger. Men with violent outbursts of anger are clearly at greater risk of death by heart attack than their calmer counterparts.[5]

In a sense, patience is maturity. One commentator notes that it is "a gift of maturity; it means rejecting the weapons which my enemy puts into my hand, and refusing to be infected by his hostility."[6] Patience gives me the intentional ability to choose my own course in life rather than letting the world dictate it.

Patience also gives me the ability to be real. I do not have all the friends I want, but I am continually coming into contact with more people with whom the possibility of friendship exists. One problem is that when many people learn that I am a minister, they feel distant from me. Ministers, these people seem to think, are not human and do not want or need friendship! I am not sure just what we preachers have done to merit such an idea. I do not know about my colleagues, but I, for one, desire and need friendship. So, for me, patience is that creative waiting as people come to know me as a real, live human being with troubles of my own and bills to pay and, I hope, a sense of humor.

John Chrysostom was a leader in the early church. He lived from about 347 until 407. He once spoke powerfully on patience.

> For it is both an invincible weapon and a sort of impregnable tower, easily beating off all annoyances: and as a spark falling into the keep doth it no injury, but is itself easily quenched, so whatever unexpected thing falls upon a long-suffering soul speedily vanishes, but the soul it disturbs not; of a truth there is nothing so impenetrable as long-suffering. You may talk of armies, money, horses, walls, arms, or anything else, you will name nothing like long-suffering; for he that is surrounded by these, being overcome by anger, is upset, like a worthless child, and fills all with confusion and tempest; but the long-suffering man, settled as it were in a harbor, enjoys a profound calm. Though he may

be surrounded with loss, the rock is not moved; though thou bruise him with stripes, thou hast not wounded the adamant. The possessor of this passive virtue hath a kind of long and noble soul, whose great strength is love.[7]

Patience does indeed make a "noble soul." As James put it, "Consider it pure joy, my brothers, whenever you face trials of many kinds, because you know that the testing of your faith develops perseverance. Perseverance must finish its work so that you may be mature and complete, not lacking anything" (James 1:2–4). The ability to wait creatively is part of God's plan for us, because we learn so much in the process.

James also spoke of patience as we wait for the Lord's return. Listen to his counsel: "Be patient, then, brothers, until the Lord's coming. See how the farmer waits for the land to yield its valuable crop and how patient he is for the autumn and spring rains. You too, be patient and stand firm, because the Lord's coming is near" (James 5:7–8).

The farmer today does all he can in one area, such as planting the crops, and then turns his attention to other matters. He sows the seed and can do no more with that, but there are animals to tend, fences to repair, machinery to maintain, financial records to keep, and a hundred other things to do. The farmer knows that patience is creative waiting. While the seeds are germinating, the farmer is working on other things.

This kind of patience is certainly not meant to make you stale. It is not intended to lead to dry rot or decay. People, like fine silverware, stay in the best shape with constant use; otherwise, both of them tend to tarnish. Thomas Hardy, in his novel *The Mayor of Casterbridge,* describes a young married couple walking down a road together, the woman holding an infant. "That the man and woman were husband and wife and the parents of the girl in arms there could be little doubt. No other than such relationship would have accounted for the atmosphere of stale familiarity which the trio carried with them . . . as they moved down the road."

"The atmosphere of stale familiarity." This is such a sad description. In no way is this what biblical patience produces. Creative waiting is not just putting up with bad situations, but it is learning and growing from them.

Eric Liddell was the Olympic runner portrayed in the movie *Chariots of Fire*. He was a Christian missionary who became a prisoner of war at Weihsien in China during the Second World War. Whole families were interned there, and the restive teenagers especially had a hard time. They resorted to sexual orgies. When Liddell became aware of this situation, he decided to take action. He did not try to establish unworkable curfews or other strictures. Instead, he and other missionaries began to structure evening programs of entertainment, supervised dances, playing games, and lessons in science and languages. One of the prisoners who would pass the "game room" in the camp would see "as often as not Eric . . . bent over a chessboard or a model boat, or directing some sort of square dance—absorbed, warm, and interested, pouring all of himself into this effort to capture the minds and imaginations of those penned-up youths."[8]

This is the meaning of Christian patience. No one wanted to be in that POW camp, but since they were, they needed to live like persons formed in the image of God rather than as animals. Liddell and others practiced the art of creative waiting—patience—and worked to better themselves and occupy their time and their minds. Liddell died of a brain tumor while still a POW, but I am sure he had no regrets. James 1:3 states that the testing of one's faith brings patience. The prisoners at Weihsien learned the truth of James's statement.

The apostle Paul probably wrote his letter to the Ephesians from a prison cell. One would think that he would be angry, bitter, resentful, and nearly dying to get out. But consider his counsel to his brothers and sisters in Ephesus: "As a prisoner for the Lord, then, I urge you to live a life worthy of the calling you have received. Be completely humble and gentle; be patient, bearing with one another in love. Make every effort to keep the unity of the Spirit through the bond of peace" (Eph. 4:1–3).

Can you imagine a prisoner telling free people to be patient? It seems laughable, but this is exactly what happened. Paul could do this because at the deepest level he, too, was free. His soul, his mind, and his imagination were all free. Only his body was captive. Paul lived patience as creative waiting. If he could not go to see his friends in Ephesus, at least he could write.

Think of this for a while. You cannot do everything you want to. (If you can, then you have your sights set too low!) But you can do so many other things. Perhaps, like Paul and Eric Liddell, you need to begin doing what you can do instead of fretting over what you cannot do. Maybe you need to write or call some people who need to hear from you. Maybe you need to practice the art of creative waiting by volunteering some of your time to vital community activities while you anticipate other things to come. As the writer of Hebrews put it, "We do not want you to become lazy, but to imitate those who through faith and patience inherit what has been promised" (Heb. 6:12).

Patience is the power to accept life's hard knocks without falling apart. Every person is caught in circumstances he did not choose. Every person has problems she would rather do without. But life is no cafeteria line where we choose only what looks good. Sometimes we get liver on our plate when we would rather have lobster.

The inability to accept life as it is leads to mental distress of the highest order. Ty Cobb, the legendary baseball player, had a lifetime batting average of .335. He stole 892 bases, made 4,191 hits, scored 2,245 runs, and batted .367 from 1905 until 1928. Cobb seemingly had so much going for him. But a sports writer summed him up thus: "His talents for collecting base hits was equaled only by a perverted genius for alienating people. So to hear Cobb described by his peers as the game's greatest player is a most telling tribute, because most of the encomiasts despised him, usually with evidence in hand, because Ty at one time or another had spiked them, turned them down, slugged them, bedeviled them, insulted them, or otherwise unsettled their digestive tracts."[9]

Two of his sons, Ty Jr. and Herschel, died before Cobb. At the age of seventy-one, Cobb tried to move back to his old home near Cornelia, Georgia. He wanted to settle down but could not. He crisscrossed the country several more times searching for peace and happiness, but he never found it. Cobb apparently could not accept life with its family tragedies. As age caught up with him, he became a manager instead of a player, but he never matched the success he had enjoyed before.

I am sympathetic with Cobb and the millions of other people just like him. They spend a lifetime running and searching for the "something" that is hard to describe, but they never find it. These people do not know the power of creative waiting, which the Bible calls patience.

John Milton, a poet who lived between 1608 and 1674, wrote a poem on his blindness. The last line has become familiar to many people, but the entire poem speaks of patience.

> When I consider how my light is spent
> Ere half my days in this dark world and wide,
> And that one talent which is death to hide
> Lodged with me useless, though my soul more bent
>
> To serve therewith my Maker, and present
> My true account, lest He returning chide.
> "Doth God exact day-labour, light denied?"
> I fondly ask. But Patience, to prevent
>
> That murmur, soon replies, "God doth not need
> Either man's work or his own gifts. Who best
> Bear his mild yoke, they serve him best. His state
>
> "Is kingly: thousands at his bidding speed,
> And post o'er land and ocean without rest;
> They also serve who only stand and wait."

Sometimes all we can do is "stand and wait." But Milton was right. That, too, can be service to God. Isaiah tells us that "they who wait for the LORD shall renew their strength" (Isa. 40:31 RSV). The word *wait* here means to twist together as a rope. Isaiah is saying that those who intertwine their lives with the life of God are the ones who are strengthened. This, certainly, is patience as creative waiting.

Consider an ancient story about a rabbi named Hillel. He lived about 20 B.C. and was considered the most patient of all the teachers at that time. Two men wagered that whoever could make Hillel angry and lose his patience would receive four hundred Zuz. So one of the men said, "I will make him angry."

It was Sabbath eve, and Hillel was washing his hair. The man went to Hillel's house and shouted at the door, "Is Hillel in? Is Hillel in?"

Hillel dressed himself and confronted the man and asked, "What do you wish, my son?"

The man answered, "I wish to ask you a question."

"You may ask it, my son," replied Hillel.

"Why are the heads of Babylonians round?"

"You have asked a great question, my son," answered Hillel. "Because the midwives of the Babylonians are not very experienced."

The man waited an hour and came back and shouted: "Is Hillel in? Is Hillel in?"

Hillel dressed again and went out to him: "What do you wish, my son?"

"I wish to ask a question."

"Ask, my son."

"Why are the eyes of the Tadmorenes [natives of Palmyra] inflamed?"

"You have asked a great question," replied Hillel. "Because they live in sandy places."

The man waited another hour, went back, and again shouted, "Is Hillel in? Is Hillel in?"

Hillel dressed again and went out to him. "What do you wish, my son?"

"I have a question to ask."

"Ask, my son," replied the rabbi.

"Why are the feet of the Africans broad?"

"You have asked a great question, my son," answered Hillel. "Because they live in watery marshes."

Then the man said, "I have many questions to ask you, but fear that you will become angry." Whereupon Hillel adjusted his robes and sat down near him and said, "Ask all the questions you have to ask."

Then the man said, "Are you Hillel that is prince of Israel? If it is you, then there should be no more men like you in Israel."

"Why?" asked Hillel.

"Because I lost four hundred Zuz because of you."

Hillel said, "Be careful of your temper. Hillel is worth the loss of four hundred Zuz and many times four hundred; but you cannot make Hillel lose his patience."[10]

Learning patience is always costly. It costs a life given to Christ for the grafting in of this fruit of the Spirit. Do you have the time?

The greatest thing a man can do for his heavenly
Father is to be kind to some of His other children.
—Henry Drummond

Chapter 5

Ethics of the Second Mile

K I N D N E S S

[handwritten: Compassion (founding of the Red Cross)]

A Swiss banker named Henri Dunant went to Italy on business in 1859. While there, he witnessed the bloody battle of Solferino on June 24. When the armies withdrew, they left their wounded on the battlefield. Dunant organized the nearby villagers for rescuing and nursing them. They tended these wounded men for weeks. Later, Dunant wrote a book asking why some international agency could not be organized to care for such people. From that incident, the Red Cross was born.[1] One man was moved by compassion and helped people who could not help themselves. His action easily fits the definition of one of the aspects of the fruit of the Spirit—kindness.

Most people seem to know intuitively that there are times to do things for people with no thought of reward or advantage. We do things because they are right to do. Period. No explanation or debate. Some psychologists call this "prosocial behavior." One scientist, Morton Hunt, speaks of "behavior carried out to benefit another at some sacrifice to oneself, and without, or not primarily because of, the expectation of rewards from external sources."[2]

Kindness is an attitude that results in action toward other people. I say, "The other person is as important as I am. I will treat him with dignity and respect. I will help him and look out for his interests as best I can."

This counsel might seem to some people like the proverbial "fiddling while Rome burns." Can you imagine saying to the leader of Iraq, "Now, Mr. Hussein, you must be kind"? Some people would consider kindness a dispensable notion. But that Jesus of Nazareth considered it an absolute necessity is equally obvious.

Jesus said on one occasion, "If someone wants to sue you and take your tunic, let him have your cloak as well. If someone forces you to go one mile, go with him two miles" (Matt. 5:40–41).

"Going the extra mile" is a phrase that has gained general usage in our society. It signifies doing more than is required, of exceeding the minimum. Kindness is the ethic of the second mile. It is the willingness to do more for others than might be required in any given circumstance. As such, it is the basis for all strong and healthy relationships.

The Kindness of God

On the whole, the Bible proclaims that God is for people. Paul put it this way when speaking of Christ: "For the Son of God, Jesus Christ, who was preached among you by me and Silas and Timothy, was not 'Yes' and 'No,' but in him it has always been 'Yes.' For no matter how many promises God has made, they are 'Yes' in Christ" (2 Cor. 1:19–20a).

Consider that. God says "Yes" to us! Out of his eternal kindness, God really loves us and affirms us. That is gospel—supreme good news.

In another place, Paul spoke of the great mercy of God toward people: "But because of his great love for us, God, who is rich in mercy, made us alive with Christ even when we were dead in transgressions—it is by grace you have been saved. And God raised us up with Christ and seated us with him in the heavenly realms in Christ Jesus, in order that in the coming ages he might show the incomparable riches of his grace, expressed in his kindness to us in Christ Jesus" (Eph. 2:4–7).

Paul knew of God's kindness, but he never thought of it as indulgence or apathy on God's part. He warned the Christians in Rome to consider together both the sternness and the kindness of God. In speaking of people as being like grafted branches, Paul noted that some branches did not grow but broke off. They broke themselves off, and God's sternness is shown toward them. The grafting took hold for others, however, and Paul said that the kindness of God is shown toward them provided that they continue in that kindness (see Rom. 11:11–24).

Isaiah had proclaimed this good news, too. He spoke of God's great compassion upon His people:

> I will tell of the kindnesses of the LORD,
>   the deeds for which he is to be praised,
>   according to all the LORD had done for us—
> yes, the many good things he has done
>   for the house of Israel,
>   according to his compassion and many
> kindnesses. (63:7)

Isaiah had wrestled all his life to understand God. He had known the power, the majesty, and the strength of God, but he also came to know His kindness. The Old Testament understanding of this aspect of God's character is unique. Other religions of the ancient Near East conceived of many kinds of gods, such as Isis and Ra. But these religions thought of their deities as capricious, fickle, or even, in some cases, untrustworthy. But the Bible calls the Lord a God who is kind.

This kindness was why God could forgive and lead His people back to Himself. The prophet Nehemiah spoke of the history of his people as they would forsake God, get into difficulty, repent, and then be brought back to Him. "And when they cried out to you again, you heard from heaven, and in your compassion you delivered them time after time" (Neh. 9:28b).

This aspect of "time after time" sounds like my own life. Does it sound like yours? I work hard at living for God and doing what I know is right. Then when things are going smoothly, like the ancient Hebrews, I slack off. Then I get into difficulty and turn with renewed vigor to God. Thankfully, He hears and accepts me back.

The kindness of God thus leads to restored relationships. The psalmist prayed, "Remember, O LORD, your great mercy and love, for they are from of old. Remember not the sins of my youth and my rebellious ways; according to your love remember me, for you are good, O LORD" (Ps. 25:6–7). God sent His Son to restore relationships that had been broken because of sin. The meaning of the Incarnation is that God wanted to bring people back to Himself.

Think of the kindness Jesus showed people. It ranged from a general compassion for many people to specific kind acts toward individuals. When He went into towns and villages teaching and preaching, He was emotionally moved by what He found. Matthew tells us, "When he saw the crowds, he had compassion on them, because they were harassed and helpless, like sheep without a shepherd" (Matt. 9:36).

The unfortunate were special recipients of Jesus' care. On one occasion, two blind men sat by the roadside when Jesus passed by, and they called out for healing. Matthew says, "Jesus had compassion on them and touched their eyes. Immediately they received their sight and followed him" (Matt. 20:34). Many bereaved people came to know Christ's special kindness. A mother was walking in a funeral procession when Jesus approached. Luke tells the story thus: "When the Lord saw her, his heart went out to her and he said, 'Don't cry.' Then he went up and touched the coffin, and those carrying it stood still. He said, 'Young man, I say to you, get up!' The dead man sat up and began to talk, and Jesus gave him back to his mother" (Luke 7:13–15).

Even many children know that John 11:35 is the shortest verse in the Bible—"Jesus wept." Its main significance is not its length but the picture it paints of Jesus. He cared. He cared about the relationship He had with His friend Lazarus and was grieved at his death the way any friend would be. The next verse says, "Then the Jews said, 'See how he loved him!'" He cared about the sisters of Lazarus and so raised him from the dead because they depended on him.

Once Jesus felt the pain of a city that would not heed His message. "O Jerusalem, Jerusalem, you who kill the prophets and stone those sent to you, how often I have longed to gather your children together, as a hen gathers her chicks under her wings, but you were not willing" (Matt. 23:37). No one can doubt the love, compassion, and kindness of one so deeply moved by the plight of others.

Kindness Toward Others

God is kind and therefore expects His people to show a similar attitude toward others. Some anonymous person put it thus: "The ministry of kindness is a ministry which may be achieved by all men, rich and poor, learned and illiterate. Brilliance of mind and capacity for deep thinking have rendered great service to humanity, but by themselves they are impotent to dry a tear or mend a broken heart."

The Bible is rich with this same sentiment and proclaims this ethic of the second mile. Kindness is expressed through the words we speak. Words are powerful and have the power to hurt or to heal. Proverbs 15:4 says, "Kind words bring life, but cruel words crush your spirit" (TEV). Verse 23 states, "What a joy it is to find just the right word for the right occasion!" One simple act of kindness that can be shown toward others is to speak to them with soothing, caring words. Have you noticed how touchy most people seem? They are apparently hassled by others and view every person as a potential enemy. The next time you are in a checkout line somewhere with a harried clerk, speak a kind word and see what happens. Sometimes these simple, almost casual acts of kindness affect people deeply and significantly.

Martin, who lived in Tours, France, in the fourth century, was later known as St. Martin of Tours. Before becoming a Christian, he had been a Roman cavalry officer. One winter day, he was riding with his regiment through the snow and slush into the city of Amiens. Crowds gathered to watch the soldiers coming in. The army was nearly freezing because of the weather. As they passed through the city, the young officer Martin dismounted. He had seen among the crowd a poor man, almost naked and blue with cold, holding out his trembling hand for alms to buy bread. Martin took off his own cloak, drew his sword, cut it in two, and then wrapped half of it around the shivering shoulders of the beggar. He put the other half around himself, remounted, and rode off.

That night as he slept, he dreamed of the half coat and heard a voice asking him if he had ever seen it. Martin looked at it, expecting to see the beggar whom he had befriended earlier that day. But he saw no beggar, only the strong and gracious face and form of Jesus. As he stared at the vision, the crowd of peasants who had laughed at his gesture toward the beggar seemed to change into groups of the heavenly host.

St. Martin of Tours learned the truth of the statement of Jesus regarding kind acts: "When you have done it unto one of these, the least of my brethren, you have done it unto me." A seemingly extravagant act of kindness led to a life-changing encounter between Martin and God. But this is not so unusual because similar events have happened with many people. Paul told the Christian church in Colossae to wrap kindness around them as a cloak: "As God's chosen people, holy and dearly loved, clothe yourselves with compassion [and] kindness . . ." (Col. 3:12).

Oscar Wilde was a writer in Victorian England whose actions matched his name. He was sent to prison for two years for a sexual crime and was later converted to Christian faith. He wrote of an incident that happened during part of his trial that changed his life. Wilde reported,

> When I was brought down from my prison to the Court of Bankruptcy, between two policemen, _____ waited in the long dreary corridor that, before the whole crowd, whom an action so sweet and simple hushed into silence, he might gravely raise his hat to me, as, handcuffed and with bowed head, I passed him by. Men have gone to heaven for smaller things than that. It was in this spirit, and with this mode of love, that the saints knelt down to wash the feet of the poor, or stooped to kiss the leper on the cheek. I have never said one single word to him about what he did. I do not know to the present moment whether he is aware that I was even conscious of his action. It is

not a thing for which one can render formal thanks in formal words. I store it in the treasure-house of my heart. I keep it there as a secret debt that I am glad to think I can never possibly repay. . . . When wisdom has been profitless to me, philosophy barren, and the proverbs and phrases of those who have sought to give me consolation as dust and ashes in my mouth, the memory of that little, lovely, silent act of love has unsealed for me all the wells of pity, . . . and brought me out of the bitterness of lonely exile into harmony with the wounded, broken, and great heart of the world.3

The tipping of a hat as an act of kindness—isn't that a strange thing to remember? Not really! Most of us remember when someone is kind to us. This points out its power.

The psalmist was wise to pray, "Set a guard over my mouth, O LORD; keep watch over the door of my lips" (Ps. 141:3). He knew the power of the tongue for the destruction of another person's self-esteem. James knew it, too. He wrote, "The tongue also is a fire, a world of evil among the parts of the body. It corrupts the whole person, sets the whole course of his life on fire, and is itself set on fire by hell. All kinds of animals, birds, reptiles and creatures of the sea are being tamed and have been tamed by man, but no man can tame the tongue. It is a restless evil, full of deadly poison" (James 3:6–8). The one who can allow kindness, as part of the fruit of the Spirit, to control his restless tongue can do mighty things. As Proverbs puts it, "He who loves a pure heart and whose speech is gracious will have the king for his friend" (22:11).

Ralph Waldo Emerson wrote, "You can never do a kindness too soon, for you never know how soon it will be too late." How true this is! Everyone has memories, still painful perhaps, of words or acts we put off saying to or doing for someone until it was too late. I have conducted many funeral services and have run across several families who tried to assuage their guilt of neglecting "grandma" by spending hundreds of dollars on flowers. I have nothing against florists, but please—Do not wait! Do it now! Be kind to those you love! Live this day as if it were your last! If this were your last day, you would probably fall all over yourself in being gracious and loving to your family. Well, it might be your last day. But even if it is not, treat others as the Lord has treated you.

The Bible is full of narratives of people who treated others kindly in the way I am describing. Consider the following examples.

Young Joseph had been sold as a slave by his jealous brothers. But the plot did not end as they had predicted. Joseph ended up being not a lowly servant but a highly placed officer in Egypt. His brothers fell on hard times, so they went to Egypt in search of food. When they realized that Joseph was still alive, they asked, "What if Joseph holds a grudge against us and pays us back for all the wrongs we did to him?" But their younger brother answered, "'Don't be afraid. Am I in the place of God? You intended to harm me, but God intended it for good to accomplish what is now being done, the saving of many lives. So then, don't be afraid. I will provide for you and your children.' And he reassured them and spoke kindly to them" (Gen. 50:15, 19–21).

Godly midwives assisted in the births of the Hebrew slaves in Egypt. The king of Egypt had ordered that if the child who was born was a male, the midwives were to kill it. If it was a female, they could let it live. The midwives refused to follow these instructions, however. "The midwives, however, feared God and did not do what the king of Egypt had told them to do; they let the boys live. Then the king of Egypt summoned the midwives and asked them, 'Why have you done this? Why have you let the boys live?' The midwives answered Pharaoh, 'Hebrew women are not like Egyptian women; they are vigorous and give birth before the midwives arrive.'" How were these women rewarded for this kindness? "So God was kind to the midwives and the people increased and became even more numerous. And because the midwives feared God, he gave them families of their own" (Exod. 1:17–20).

A widow named Ruth and her mother-in-law Naomi journeyed back to Naomi's home in Bethlehem. They met a man named Boaz, who allowed the two women to go into his fields to pick up whatever grain the other workers left behind. Boaz ordered his men, "Even if she gathers among the sheaves, don't embarrass her. Rather, pull out some stalks for her from the bundles and leave them for her to pick up, and don't rebuke her" (Ruth 2:15–16). So Ruth gleaned in the field until late in the evening and went home with plenty to eat and even some left over. Eventually, Ruth and Boaz married and had a son who became the grandfather of David. Who knows where a simple act of kindness might lead?

When David was king of Israel, he searched for someone of Saul's family to whom he could show gratitude. A man named Mephibosheth, the son of Jonathan, who had been David's great friend, was found. He was summoned before David. "'Don't be afraid,' David said to him, 'for I will surely show you kindness for the sake of your father Jonathan. I will restore to you all the land that belonged to your grandfather Saul, and you will always eat at my table'" (2 Sam. 9:7). Some debts are long-standing but come due with much accrued interest.

Paul, on one of his many voyages, was shipwrecked. When he reached the shore, he found a pleasant surprise for himself and the others. "Once safely on shore, we found out that the island was called Malta. The islanders showed us unusual kindness. They built a fire and welcomed us all because it was raining and cold" (Acts 28:1–2). Here is simple human compassion.

Jesus once told a story of a man for whom the milk of human kindness had not soured. The man, himself a victim of discrimination and irrational hatred, traveled along a narrow road one day and found another victim. This victim, however, had been the target of muggers who had left him for dead. The fellow traveling the road waited for nothing but picked up the injured man, set him upon his donkey, and took him to an inn where he could be helped. This kind man has been immortalized in history and his very name symbolizes compassion—the good Samaritan (Luke 10:25–37). He had known hate and rejection because he was thought of as a "half breed." But he realized that hate had to seep into his heart to cause the most damage, and he refused to allow that. So one victim could feel compassion for another and act kindly toward him.

Learning the Kindness of Christ

A little girl had found a turtle in her yard one day but could not get it to come out of its shell. Her uncle watched for a while as the girl tried everything she could to coax the turtle out. Finally he said, "If you put him by the fireplace, he'll warm up after awhile and come out by himself." Then, as almost an afterthought, the uncle added, "People are sorta' like terrapins. Never try to force a fellow into anything. Just warm him up with a little human kindness, and more'n likely he'll come your way."[4]

This sort of thing comes easier for some than for others. Some people seem gifted with the ability to "warm up" others with kindness whereas the rest of us have to struggle to do it. We may not lack the desire to be kind, but we are short on technique. If so, technique can be learned to some degree. Paul wrote to the Colossians and instructed them to clothe themselves with kindness. This calls to mind an image of a person getting dressed. We can learn to "dress" ourselves with kindness.

When King Charles II gave William Penn, the Quaker, land in the New World, he also gave Penn the power to make war on the Indians. But Penn refused to build forts or have soldiers in his province. Instead, he treated the Indians kindly and treated them as equals. All disputes between the two races were settled by a meeting of six white men and six Indians. When Penn died, the Indians mourned him as a friend. After Penn's death, other colonies were constantly under attack by the Indians. But Pennsylvania was free from such attacks as long as they refused to arm themselves. Many years later, the Quakers were outvoted in the state, and the colony, giving in to pressure, began spending money to build forts and train soldiers against possible aggression. You can guess what happened. They were immediately attacked.

Learning the ethic of the second mile has its roots in childhood, of course. A child who grows up with some careful guidance in how to relate to others has a jump on one who grows up treating other children as mere nuisances. Parents must be cautious to give their children guidance in both why and how to treat others with respect. This calls for taking time with the kids. Kindness is not some "magical" virtue that falls fully grown from heaven. It must be learned, if not as a child, then as an adult. Sometimes it is the art of seeing life through another's eyes and acting on the insight.

Kindness (Random Acts of Kindness)

Professor Chuck Wall from Bakersfield College got tired of "random acts of violence." He began a campaign called "random acts of senseless kindness." He assigned his students an essay on the subject. Before long, automobile bumper stickers began showing up that read, "Today, I will commit one random act of senseless KINDNESS. . . . Will you?"[5] Another person wrote a book about performing these acts. The book, titled *Guerrilla Kindness,* says, "When we do a kindness without any regard for recognition or reward, when we inconvenience ourselves and freely give part of ourselves away, we challenge the every-man-for-himself logic of the world."[6] The author cites medical research that demonstrates the healing power of doing good. People who regularly help others develop stronger immune systems, improved cardiovascular circulation, and a heightened sense of well-being, and they also live longer. Be kind. Live longer.

Kindness is doing what you can to help others, even when it seems unconventional and unique. One lady does this in an unusual way. She volunteers to work in a children's hospital. Several times each week, this lady dresses as a clown and goes around the wards playing with the children. Even though she would rather avoid it, if possible, there are times when she encounters children in great pain who are crying. She carries popcorn with her. When she finds a child crying, she takes a kernel of popcorn and touches it to the cheek of the child to absorb the tears. Then she offers it to the child or she pops it into her mouth. Then the two of them sit for a while and eat tears. For some reason, it really helps the children.[7] Eating tears. Sharing pain. Who but the kind would do that?

Since first hearing of this clown in the children's ward, I have thought much about her. She has no medical power to stop the pain of a child who might be burned or who might have cancer. But she does have the willingness to sit where they sit and to share their pain as best she can. Ezekiel did this as he sat with the exiles in Tel Aviv. He wrote, "I came to the exiles who lived at Tel Abib near the Kebar River. And there, where they were living, I sat among them for seven days—overwhelmed" (Ezek. 3:15).

Think about your experiences. Who has helped you the most, someone who stood aloof from you and preached pious sermons, or someone who got involved in the nitty-gritty of your struggles and "ate tears" with you? There certainly is a place for sermons, but not if they are somehow divorced from the twentieth century and individual lives. A sermon that stays in first-century Palestine might be a good lecture in ancient history, but it is not the Word of God, which is alive and active and as modern as tomorrow's headlines.

Kindness is the willingness to throw in with others for a shared life. I do not mean that everyone should run out and join a commune. What I am suggesting is that we begin to see ourselves as part of a great community—the church. The early Christians knew this, but American Christianity is so individualistic that we have a difficult time understanding this concept. To be kind, in the biblical sense, is to see yourself as partially responsible both to and for others and to act accordingly.

I was in New Orleans one day and had my attention drawn to an old Chevy. Across the trunk the owner had put in large, black-taped letters: AVENGE YOURSELF—LIVE LONG ENOUGH TO BE A PROBLEM TO YOUR CHILDREN. I got a laugh out of that portable advertisement for revenge, but it reminded me of situations that are not funny. Far too many people carry grudges and resentments and even deep hatreds throughout their lives. Talk of living out the biblical meaning of kindness is meaningless where anger and hatred are the major motivating forces in a person's life. To learn kindness is to learn to forgive others. Otherwise, life will be stunted and deformed.

Robert Furey says that kind people realize something about others. "The kindest people I have ever known have all had something in common. They have all understood that people have faults. Beyond this, they accept imperfect people. It's as if they are prepared to forgive because they know that the need to forgive will surely arise again. This is not a pessimistic attitude. Indeed, it is profoundly optimistic. A human being with a forgiving way can survive and thrive in a world that sometimes hurts."[8] He is right.

Composer Frederick Chopin once went to the home of a friend and watched the family dog chase its tail around and around. Chopin went home and wrote a piece of music to accompany tail chasing. He called it "The Little Dog Waltz," but we know it today as "The Minute Waltz." I have felt at times that "The Little Dog Waltz" was the theme song for my life. At times, I seem to be spinning in circles—virtually chasing my own tail. When I halt the vertigo long enough to examine what is wrong, I usually find that my equilibrium is upset by attitudes of anger or resentment. These are such boomerang emotions. I throw them at someone else, but they always seem to come back to me. They hurt me far more than anyone else. As someone put it, "Anger is a craving for salt from someone who is dying of thirst." If we would learn to be kind, as the Bible instructs us, we will first have to cleanse ourselves of the negative attitudes and emotions that prohibit kindness.

Think about most of the situation comedies that are on television now. Most of them use put-down humor to get laughs. Put-down humor is one person insulting another or in some way putting another down. This is the simplest form of humor for TV writers to come up with, but it is also the most destructive type of humor. It strips others of their self-respect and proper love for themselves. (Remember, Jesus did say to love your neighbor as you love yourself.) The constant insulting that goes on in television under the name of humor is a very destructive force. It carries over into real life. Children and adults alike learn to think that they are sophisticated by being cynical and sarcastic toward others. But can you really believe that this is the best way to live and treat others?

One of the kindest things parents can do is to make time for their children. This sounds so obvious that it should not be said, but I am convinced that it is not obvious. I speak as a person who observes the lack of kindness of parents toward children and also as one who sometimes fails in this area. Too often we adults tend to assume that the only "important" things are what we are doing, and that the world of a child is trivial and unimportant.

Maybe we could learn from the woman who walked along a path in a city park with her daughter. As they passed the park fountain, the little girl saw the spray diffuse the sunlight into rainbows. She called this to her mother's attention. The mother told the girl to hurry before they missed their bus. But she saw the innocent joy on the face of the girl as she watched the rainbows, so this mother stopped, put her arms around the child, and they watched the rainbows together. She realized that another bus would come along, but they might never have another opportunity to watch rainbows in just this same way.[9]

My father was an oil-field hand. When I was growing up, he worked as a toolpusher—the boss—on an oil drilling rig. This job meant that he was on twenty-four-hour call. I remember many times when he would be gone from home for days at a time when some trouble at the rig necessitated his being there. He was always busy, but in his crazy schedule I seldom felt cheated or deprived of time with him. During the summers and holidays, our family would often go to the rig location with him. We lived in Louisiana, and he often had to work in Texas, so we would rent some little, low-cost house wherever he was. These were such special times for us. My older brother Glenn and I would go to the drilling site with Dad. He taught us to find things to do around there. If the rig was near a lake or bayou or river, we would fish. Dad might have only an hour or two to spare, but whatever he had he gave to us. If we were near a marsh, we would duck hunt. We never once went on a "vacation" in the sense of traveling to some location strictly for the purpose of enjoyment. My father never had that kind of time or money. But he did know how to give his attention to his children. One of the best Christmas dinners I ever had was when we went to be with my father at the rig. The rig was stacked—not operating—for the holidays and he had to stay with it to prevent thefts. My mother, sister Linda, brother Glenn, and I stayed with Dad in the bunkhouse for several days during the Christmas break from school. On Christmas Day, we ate Spam and crackers and drank Pepsi, and it was great! We were together, and I had a ball.

As I got older, I had wished to be in a family that was more "regular." I was not sure what that meant, but it had something to do with the father working a "regular" job, coming home every night, and going off for vacations like some of my friends did. Only later did I realized that we were regular. I had some mythical image in my mind about what a family should be and do. As I look back now, I realize that although my father was away much of the time, he always wanted to be home when he could and wanted us to be with him when we could. Many of my friends whom I considered "regular" never did half the things I did, never traveled half as much, and never felt the special love and kindness of a father as I did. Sure, times were tough and money was sometimes in short supply, but we never once missed a meal. The dinner at the rig of Spam and Pepsi, the early morning hunting expeditions, the evening fishing trips—these and a hundred events like them blended together into a life that was in many ways idyllic.

My wife, Carla, grew up in a bit different manner. Her father was a self-employed salesman for a small company. She and her family moved around a great deal and never had much money to spare. But her parents, Carl and Betty, made life an adventure and fun. They gave themselves to Carla and her older sister Diane. That is the key. Children need the love and concern—which is what kindness is—of parents. The rest, such as a fancy house, a big car, an annual vacation, and so on, are just fluff and unnecessary for real happiness.

Make the best of what you now have. Show your children rainbows. If you cannot have turkey and dressing, then eat Spam and Pepsi, but do it with a sense of adventure and love and kindness. If you cannot vacation at Yellowstone National Park, then keep your eyes open for the marvels of nature and places of historical interest in your own area. Most of us "ordinary" people miss so much of what we can see and do because we concentrate on what we cannot have. Change the way you look at things. Concentrate on what you already have and can do. Be kind to yourself. You deserve it!

Try a little kindness. It really is good advice for all of us, but for Christians it is more than good advice. It is an ethical imperative. Jesus taught an ethic of the second mile, doing more than is necessary, giving instead of only trying to get. People need what you have to offer. It is the ethic of the second mile.

*Goodness consists not in the outward things we do,
but in the inward thing we are. To be good is a
great thing.*

—Edwin Hubbell Chapin

Chapter 6

For Goodness' Sake

G O O D N E S S

A STORY IS TOLD ABOUT two men who moved to the desert to devote themselves to holy living and prayer. The two hermits lived together in the same hut but had never had even the slightest disagreement. One said to the other, "Let us have one quarrel, the way other men do."

The second answered, "But I do not know how one makes a quarrel."

The first replied, "Look, I will set a tile between us and say, 'That is mine,' and you say, 'It is mine,' and in this way trouble and contention will arise."

They agreed to do this. They set the tile between them and the first holy man said, "It is mine."

The second replied, "I hope that it is mine."

To which the first answered, "If it is yours, take it." After that, they could find no way of quarreling.[1]

Holy hermits living in the desert may not be able to find much to quarrel about, but the rest of us are not so lucky! Strife seems to be our middle name. Any two people being together seem to be like flint and steel to make sparks. Yet most people really do want to get along with others. The inability to get along with others has wreaked havoc on both personal and international levels. On the personal level, it has injured or even ended careers of people who seemed very promising.

Dr. William Menninger has found some remarkable statistics regarding people who have been fired from their jobs in industry. Social incompetence accounts for 60 to 80 percent of the failures. Only about 20 to 40 percent are due to technical incompetence.[2] Who can estimate the destruction caused on an international level because people have difficulty getting along?

Paul said that part of the fruit of the Spirit is goodness. This is not a false, self-conscious, or forced "goodness." Instead, Paul had in mind something close to generosity.[3] It is the ability to give, to give in, to reach out, and to care. It is the inner structure of moral life and ethical thought.

We might think of a person's interior and emotional life as being like a bank account. If one is "in the black" with something in reserve, one can be generous and loving. But if one's inner account is "in the red" and running a deficit, one will have nothing left to give. Many people have deep-seated emotional problems. How can someone who is emotionally bankrupt be good in the sense of being generous in his or her attitudes and actions toward others?

Finding Inner Goodness

Paul was not thinking of someone who is "goody-goody." No one likes such a person. I have a friend who says he has a good "BD"—Baloney Detector. He has the ability to sniff out insincerity in someone at 100 yards. He can tell when someone is putting on a front and when that person is being genuine. Actually, the church would be better off if everyone had a good "BD." (Theological seminaries used to give BDs—Bachelor of Divinity degrees, but that is another story.)

Of course, not everyone even likes genuine goodness. Do you remember the old television program *All in the Family*? The central characters were Archie and Edith Bunker. One evening, the two of them had the following conversation:

Archie: That's you all right, Edith the Good. You'll
           stoop to anything to be good. You never yell.
           You never swear. You never make nobody
           mad. You think it's easy living with a saint?
           Even when you cheat, you don't cheat to
           win. You cheat to lose. Edit', you ain't hu-
           man.

Edith: That's a terrible thing to say, Archie Bunker.
           I am just as human as you are.

Archie: Oh yeah? Then prove you're just as human
           as me. Do something rotten.[4]

Poor Edith's dilemma is similar to that of many other people, some of whom are reading this book. Some of you reading this book live around people, perhaps close family, who do not have the same outlook on life as you do. You feel the dialogue between Archie and Edith as a stinging reminder that even when you try doing your best and being all you can be, some people misunderstand. They mock or jeer or, maybe even worse, hold your ideals to scorn. Appropriating the fruit of the Spirit known as goodness is no simple task. It never has been. The best Man who ever lived was motivated by His inner love, generosity, and concern for people as well as by His devotion to His heavenly Father. But those inner ideals were not enough to keep our spiritual ancestors from spiking that good Man to a cross.

I find it a great mystery that people who value excellence on the football field seem to care nothing about excellence on the moral gridiron. During a recent Super Bowl, an estimated eighty-five million people watched two teams who were supposed to be the best. Kicking, running, passing, blocking, and other moves were executed to their highest possible level. Why would not these same eighty-five million people tune in to watch a special program about men, women, and children who have demonstrated a spirit of excellence in the moral and ethical aspects of life?

There are many answers to this question, of course, but one of them has to do with the aversion people have toward genuinely good people. Why does Archie resent Edith's goodness? Why do the spouses of some of you who are reading this book resent your generous approach to others? Part of the reason is that your attitude threatens them, and no one likes to feel threatened.

Paul wrote to his young friend Titus about the grace of God: "It teaches us to say 'No' to ungodliness and worldly passions, and to live self-controlled, upright and godly lives in this present age, while we wait for the blessed hope—the glorious appearing of our great God and Savior, Jesus Christ, who gave himself for us to redeem us from all wickedness and to purify for himself a people that are his very own, *eager to do what is good*" (Titus 2:12–14, italics added). To live in Christ is to live in the desire and the ability for goodness in its deepest meaning—goodness as part of who I am and not just what I do.

We find inner goodness through the inner transformation that occurs in our relationship with Christ. This is a lifelong process that is never complete. It is a goal toward which to move, but one that in this life is never fully reached. This fact need not cause despair. I simply realize that I will never attain full inner goodness on this planet. I am too flawed, too hemmed in by my own weaknesses and problems. My hope is that I look to Christ who is "the author and perfecter of our faith" (Heb. 12:2). To find genuine inner goodness, we must avoid a false variety.

Avoid Shortsighted "Goodness"

People have the right to be repulsed by people who mistake their own prudish or shortsighted views for the voice of the Almighty. In 1800, a small pamphlet titled "Excerpt from the Memoirs of Caroline E. Smelt" was published. Miss Smelt, it seems, was an insufferable prude who thought of herself as the paragon of virtue. On her deathbed, she sent the following message to her cousin: "Tell her never to enter a theatre, never to play cards, never to attend tea parties. For if any one of these is evil, they all are; and of this I am absolutely certain."[5]

The world is full of such people—always ready to pass judgment on everyone else and on every activity based on their own limited views of life. The Scriptures promise that the Christian is free in Christ and that Jesus gives an abundant life (John 10:10). He paid a high price for me, and I refuse to allow the Caroline Smelts of this world—however well-meaning they might appear—to squeeze my mind into their purses or briefcases. No wonder Henry David Thoreau once wrote, "If I knew . . . that a man was coming to my house with the conscious design of doing me good, I should run for my life."

Freedom in Christ gives freedom for good as well as freedom from evil. Paul wrote about the confidence that comes from a relationship with Christ: "Such confidence as this is ours through Christ before God. Not that we are competent in ourselves to claim anything for ourselves, but our competence comes from God. He had made us competent as ministers of a new covenant—not of the letter but of the Spirit; *for the letter kills, but the Spirit gives life*" (2 Cor. 3:4–6, italics added).

Goodness is not a sugary, sticky, false goodness that is actually a retreat from life. Jesus had constant battles with people who thought of themselves as good. They were called Pharisees. They thought that they knew all there was to know about faith and, therefore, that God was in their back pockets. But the Scriptures tell us that the very ones who thought they were the wisest, the most intelligent, and the most deserving of God's attention were the ones who had misunderstood the most!

Every generation has its own form of pharisaism—an attitude that sets itself up as judge and jury of every issue. For example, you can turn on television any Sunday morning and hear a variety of preachers speaking about every imaginable issue. The medium of television is powerful and makes these ministers seem more knowledgeable than they really are. As one woman once said to me, "If these people are on television, they must know what they are talking about." Perhaps. But perhaps not. Any time a person uses the pulpit to tell others, in no uncertain terms, what to think about every matter under heaven and how to act, that is an illegitimate use of power. God gave each of us brains and expects us to use them.

I take very seriously the declarations of the Bible about evil.

Therefore, I am always suspicious of people who act and talk as if they themselves have no taint of troubles, problems, or sin. Certainly I want people to develop and display goodness as part of the fruit of the Spirit of God. But what I do not want is to see people merely fooling themselves into believing that they have somehow overcome all temptation and that they always act from only the purest motives. The irony of all of this is that the one who thinks he is good probably is not. A well-known theologian thought much about this matter and wrote,

> Folly is a more dangerous enemy to the good than evil. One can protest against evil; it can be unmasked and, if need be, prevented by force. Evil always carries the seeds of its own destruction, as it makes people, at the least, uncomfortable. Against folly we have no defense. Neither protests nor force can touch it; reasoning is no use; facts that contradict personal prejudices can simply be disbelieved—indeed, the fool can counter by criticizing them, and if they are undeniable, they can just be pushed aside as trivial exceptions. So the fool, as distinct from the scoundrel, is completely self-satisfied; in fact, he can easily become dangerous, as it does not take much to make him aggressive. A fool must therefore be treated more cautiously than a scoundrel; we shall never again try to convince a fool by reason, for it is both useless and dangerous.[6]

This is all a bit touchy, so let me recap for a moment. The Bible tells us that part of the fruit of the Spirit of God is goodness. Goodness is a quality of life that begins on the inside and moves to the outside. It is marked with a high quality of self-awareness and truthfulness. A genuinely good person does not go around all the time playing Little Jack Horner—"see what a good boy am I." Goodness is open to growth and correction precisely because it knows it has not arrived yet. Goodness that pretends perfection is false and dangerous. As the Scriptures put it, "Pride goes before destruction, a haughty spirit before a fall" (Prov. 16:18). Goodness is never satisfied with itself nor proud of its achievements but is forever on the lookout for new growth, new understanding, and new ways to change more into the image of the Master. Above all, it is not false or a pretense.

A good man or woman, in the biblical sense, always seeks to model his or her life after Jesus, who "went around doing good" (Acts 10:38). And a good person neither makes excuses for his or her failures nor blames them on others. The good person does not injure others through words or deeds and then try to get out of it by saying, "God told me to say this," or "The Lord made me do this."

A psychologist who works closely with people who seek his help noticed this tendency to offer excuses. He wrote,

> On our pilgrimage, we are defeated not only by the narrowness of our perspective, and our fear of the darkness, but by our excuses as well. How often we make circumstances our prison, and other people our jailers. If only I were not married, or if at least my wife were not so cautious, what great ventures I could pursue. Translation: It's a good thing my wife takes responsibility for reminding me of the hazards of some undertakings; otherwise I might plunge headlong into the abyss. In this way I can act with realistic caution, while maintaining the image of myself as the undaunted adventurer. But, too, in this way I sometimes forgo recognizing the extent of my freedom, timidly avoid some situations that frighten me, and make excuses for my constraint. At my best, I take full responsibility for what I do and for what I choose not to do. I see that there is no prison except that which I construct to protect myself from feeling my pain, from risking my losses.[7]

One way to find out what God wants is to realize what He forbids. The Ten Commandments offer good guidance here, although these commandments are not primarily negative. Next, search the Scriptures to find the major sections that offer guidance on what God requires. The Sermon on the Mount in Matthew 5 through 7 is very helpful here. Further, look at the New Testament teaching on spiritual gifts. The Spirit gives Christians specific gifts. Part of knowing God's will for our lives is to consider these gifts and to learn which one(s) are present. Then the task is to cultivate them and put them into practice. Beyond this, let me communicate something very vital about our knowledge of God. God is bigger than any of our ideas about Him. He calls us to a life of courageous action. To be a Christian is not to retreat from life and hide from its pains. It is, instead, to live in the freedom for good things.

The Courage to Be Good

We need moral and intellectual courage to cultivate the fruit of the Spirit known as goodness. To be a coward and hide from life takes no courage and very little effort. The trouble with that, though, is that you end up at the finish of your life with nothing to show for your days.

I do not want to spend my life hiding from imagined pain. I do not want to waste my energy, which is renewable but still limited, watching television all the time when I could talk to neighbors, write letters to friends, play games with my children, or expand my mind with a good book. More than this, though, I do not want to dodge my responsibility as a member of the community by refusing to work in my community for its betterment. Goodness is a virtue that leads us to get involved with people and their troubles as well as their triumphs.

I am convinced that one of the reasons why the church does not do a better job of winning people to Christ is that many people see Christians as basically selfish. Folks outside the church sometimes think of Christians as weaklings who have "feathered their nests" with the belief that they are special to "their God," as it is sometimes put. They note the absence of Christians in some areas of life, such as politics and peacemaking ventures, and wonder why, if Christ makes people stronger and better, these Christians do not get more involved in life. After all, do not these Christians tell of a Christ who refused to stay in a privileged place in heaven but chose to come live in the rough-and-tumble world of people?

Herman Melville, best known as the author of *Moby Dick,* once wrote of a commodore on a warship, "It beseemed him . . . to erect himself into an example of virtue, and show the gun-deck what virtue was. But alas! when Virtue sits high aloft on a frigate's poop, when Virtue is crowned in the cabin a commodore, when Virtue rules by compulsion, and domineers over Vice as a slave, then Virtue, though her mandates be outwardly observed, bears little interior sway. To be efficacious, Virtue must come down from aloft, even as our blessed Redeemer came down to redeem our whole man-of-war world; to that end, mixing with its sailors and sinners as equals."[8]

When "goodness" sees itself as the paragon of virtue and goes out to prove itself good, it usually ends up doing the opposite. When this "goodness" heads out on a witch-hunt, it often bags the wrong quarry.

You cannot read the New Testament without coming to the conclusion that the writers believed that something is fundamentally wrong with people. The Bible calls that something "sin." Some people today suggest that all that is wrong with people is that they live in a bad environment, or that their subconscious mind is making them behave badly, or that they simply have not yet learned how to act correctly.

All of these factors do affect behavior, of course. But are they the major factors in human nature? I do not think so. The Scriptures say that a person must be born again, must repent of sin, must be spiritually remade by God. This is not a view of a human nature that suggests that it is slightly flawed, but rather that something is dramatically and tragically defective. I take this view seriously.

To appropriate the biblical meaning of goodness, then, requires an inner transformation of a person. If you have never had this happen, I urge you to talk to a minister or a person you know is a serious Christian. One of these people can tell you how to experience this inner transformation. The New Testament calls this change salvation. It is not just for a select few, but for any who wish to be related to God through faith.

A very brilliant man who lived earlier in this century was both a gifted musician and a formidable philosopher. His name was Albert Schweitzer. When he was about thirty, Schweitzer began to wrestle with a decision about giving up his career as a musician and professor to enter medical school and become a missionary doctor. He felt keenly the call of God to go to the Congo to help the people there, and he realized that the best way he could help was by becoming a doctor. One would think that Schweitzer's friends would have supported his decision and helped any way they could. Such was not the case, however. He wrote about this in his autobiography.

> My thirtieth birthday, a few months later, I spent like the man in the parable who "desiring to build a tower, first counts the cost whether he have wherewith to complete it." The result was that I resolved to realize my plan of direct human service in Equatorial Africa. With the exception of one trustworthy friend no one knew of my intention. When it became known through the letters I had sent from Paris, I had hard battles to fight with my relations and friends. Almost more than with my contemplated new start itself they reproached me with not having shown them so much confidence as to discuss it with them first. With this side issue they tormented me beyond measure during those difficult weeks. That theological friends should outdo the others in their protests struck me as all the more preposterous, because they had, no doubt, all preached a fine sermon—perhaps a very fine one—showing how St. Paul, as he has recorded in his letter to the Galatians, "conferred not with flesh and blood" beforehand about what he meant to do for Jesus.
>
> My relatives and my friends all joined in expostulating with me on the folly of my enterprise. I was a man, they said, who was burying the talent entrusted to him and wanted to trade with false currency. Work among savages I ought to leave to those who would not thereby be compelled to leave gifts and acquirements in science and art unused.
>
> I had assumed as a matter of course that familiarity with the sayings of Jesus would produce a much better

appreciation of what to popular logic is nonrational, than my own case had allowed me to assert.[9]

This is really amazing, isn't it? Schweitzer's friends and family, and especially his religious friends, balked at the thought of his going to Africa. They thought he was going to "waste" his life. He had to act courageously to cultivate goodness as part of the fruit of the Spirit of God in his life.

All of this takes great courage. We might as well face the fact that we cannot be good without being courageous. Goodness is both inner moral strength and outward ethical action. No wonder the New Testament says that God gives this through His Spirit. This is nothing that can be manufactured on demand. A doctor thought about this matter of courage, especially among some of his patients, and noted:

> Life is beautiful, but it is hard for all human beings, very hard even for the majority. It is even harder in misfortune, in the face of deprivation. That requires a lot of courage. I stress that fact because I am well aware that it is something of which I have very little. My own courage revives when I come into contact with courageous people—often my patients, more handicapped than I am, and displaying courage which I admire. For courage is not taught, it is caught. Society is a vast laboratory of mutual encouragement. Each member can give the other only the courage he has himself—doctors as well as patients.[10]

Goodness and Its Opposite

When it comes down to it, we do not need definitions. We can simply see goodness and its opposite if we keep our eyes open. Let me tell you about something that happened to me. You will see what I mean.

Do you wonder why some people hunker in darkness while others revel in the light? You have seen both types. What about a girl whose whole being telegraphs, "I know God and am loved despite life's setbacks"? What about a man who has had chance after chance and still chooses to shrivel up instead of grow in goodness? I saw them both back to back. A new job had taken me from Louisiana to Memphis and I was "batching" for a few weeks until my family could join me. I got weary of peanut butter and tuna fish so one night I went to a local restaurant for dinner. The waiter seated me at a small table for one against a half wall. A couple was seated across the half wall but were on a higher level than I was. Because of that arrangement the man seemed to be speaking into my left ear. I wasn't trying to eavesdrop, but I simply could not help overhearing the conversation.

I was in the market for a house, so I had a real estate book with me. As I read the ads for houses, the voices of the couple next to me became persistent. They were obviously on a date. Both of them were probably in their mid- to late-thirties. When I sat down, the first thing I heard was a vulgar question the man asked the woman. She was embarrassed and offended. The man seemed not to notice and pressed on.

I did not like what I was hearing but thought I could ignore them. I kept reading: "Nice four-bedroom, two-bath house on half acre lot. . . ."

The man's voice sliced into my consciousness again. He began to tell his date all about himself although she never asked. His previous question had turned her off like a switch, but he was too full of himself to notice.

He explained that he had been married and divorced three times. He said that he did not always get along too well with women. Now there was an understatement! He admitted having been unfaithful with his first and third wives. In a bid to gain some sympathy points, he explained he had been faithful to his second wife. Of course, that marriage lasted only a year and a half. From his tone, I could tell that he thought that all of that was funny. From her silence, I could tell that she did not. Since the stories of his nuptial disasters did not impress his date, he changed tactics.

I kept reading: "Lovely two-story house with large great room and fireplace. Perfect for family gatherings. . . ."

The voice cut through again. He told her all about the tragedies he had experienced—a brother who was killed in Vietnam and his father who died at about the same time. Business failures were dragged in, too. He had been bankrupt once.

On and on it went. Was he out for sympathy? I thought he needed it.

I kept reading: "Nonqualifying assumable mortgage on nice county property perfect for construction. . . ."

The voice again. He explained how he was an easygoing guy who liked everybody and got on well with people. In the next breath, he told how one of his ex-wives had done something to anger him, so he sneaked into her yard one night and poured gasoline all over the grass to kill it. "I showed her," he crowed.

Yes, I thought, *you showed her, and you are showing your date, too. But what are you showing her?*

He bragged about making an anonymous call to the man his former wife was seeing at the time and lying about having an affair with her just to upset them both.

My real estate book seemed more and more interesting with each passing minute. Finally, the couple finished their meal and left. Mr. Manners walked off and left his date to trail along behind. I thought, *You won't ever need to ask her out again.*

That man seemed to be a black hole—so dense that no light could escape from him. He had everything but made nothing out of it. I noticed. His date did, too.

The next day, I took a flight out from Memphis to Dallas. The flight was packed, and the airline asked if anyone would give up a seat for cash and a ticket on a later flight. I had plenty of time to make connections, so I volunteered. When everyone else was seated, the stewardess told me there was one more seat. She sat me next to a girl with Down's syndrome. Apparently, no one else wanted to sit there since the seat next to her was the only empty seat on the plane. I did not mind because I have been around people with Down's syndrome before and found them to be delightful.

The girl looked to be in her late teens. I decided to help her if she needed it, but she did not. She had a ball! Whatever came up, she handled. She sighed and hummed and had a great time watching clouds and drinking diet cola. Then she noticed that the blue seat cover in front of her had some brown rectangle designs. Five or six times, the girl's stubby index finger of her right hand punched the designs as she counted: "One, two, three, four . . ." Then she double-checked the count on the fingers of her left hand. Her concentration was intense. Her brow furrowed as she continued, "Five, six, seven, eh, seven, eight . . ." More finger work. More concentration: "Nine, ten, eleven, twelve," and then a sigh of relief as she counted the last two: ". . . thirteen, fourteen." She beamed in triumph. I beamed a little, too. A few minutes later, she started all over again. It was as if the whole world depended on her counting those fourteen brown rectangles on blue fabric.

An older man met her in Dallas. He looked like he might be her grandfather. She laughed and cried as she grabbed him, and he laughed and cried. I can't explain why, but I laughed and cried, too. That little girl radiated the light of God and reveled in life.

Two chance encounters. One with someone who seemed to relish the darkness; one with someone who lived in all the light that she could understand. One who seemed to be headed to what C. S. Lewis once described as hell—a tiny place between two blades of grass where a person must spend his whole life getting small enough to go there; one who loved and laughed and was proud of small achievements.

We are given choices in life. Some of us have many options whereas others have few. Either way, we choose. We can live in the light or, if we really, really want to, we can choose to ignore the light and to live in the darkness. At the restaurant and on the plane, I encountered one who did each. God knows which is which.

God grant that we might acquire the courage to be good. God grant, too, that we rub elbows with genuinely good people, for goodness, like courage, is not taught but caught.

Without faithfulness, we are like stained glass
windows in the dark.

—Anonymous

Chapter 7

Held in Firm Grip

FAITHFULNESS

WILLIAM CULLEN BRYANT'S well-known poem "Thanatopsis" pictures a person going to his death with courage because of the way he has lived:

> So live, that when thy summons comes to join
> The innumerable caravan which moves
> To that mysterious realm, where each shall take
> His chamber in the silent halls of death,
> Thou go not, like a quarry-slave at night,
> Scourged to his dungeon, but, sustained and soothed
> By unfaltering trust, approach thy grave
> Like one who wraps the drapery of his couch
> About him, and lies down to pleasant dreams.

This is a magnificent picture, but it makes us ask, "How can I live this way?" Paul gives us a clue when he speaks of part of the fruit of the Spirit as "faithfulness." You and I can reach the end of life with the confidence expressed in the poem by being faithful to our Lord, to our families, and especially to ourselves.

The word *faithfulness* in the original language is *pistis,* and it is translated as "faith" in some older versions of the Bible. But most newer versions translate it as in Galatians 5:22—"faithfulness." William Barclay explains clearly the reason for this translation. He notes that faith means

> absolute trust, absolute self-surrender, absolute confidence, absolute obedience in regard to Jesus Christ. This is what might be called a theological virtue; it is rather the basis of belief and the basis of our whole relationship to God through Jesus Christ. But the virtues listed in the fruit of the Spirit are not theological virtues; they are ethical virtues: they have to do not so much with our relationship to God as with our relationship to our fellow-men. What *pistis* here means is not faith but faithfulness; it is the quality of reliability, trustworthiness, which makes a man a person on whom we can utterly rely and whose word we can utterly accept.[1]

Barclay's explanation helps us understand what Paul is trying to communicate. This trustworthiness and reliability is an inner strength and quality of one who yields his or her life to the Spirit of God. The person with the quality of faithfulness can be counted on and trusted.

Jesus spoke of those who tried artificial or external means of ensuring the truthfulness of their word by swearing oaths. Jesus' prohibition against oaths points out that no external binder can make a dishonest person honest. Jesus said, "Again, you have heard that it was said to the people long ago, 'Do not break your oath, but keep the oaths you have made to the Lord.' But I tell you, Do not swear at all: either by heaven, for it is God's throne; or by the earth, for it is his footstool; or by Jerusalem, for it is the city of the Great King. And do not swear by your head, for you cannot make even one hair white or black. Simply let your 'Yes' be 'Yes,' and your 'No,' 'No'; anything beyond this comes from the evil one" (Matt. 5:33–37).

I once knew a man who was a notorious liar. No one believed anything he said because he seemed to prefer a lie to the truth. Whenever he would try to convince someone of his honesty, he would add the kicker, "I swear on my mother's grave." I think of this fellow when I remember Jesus' words about letting my "Yes" be "Yes" and my "No" be "No." Jesus wants His followers to be true to their word. If my inner life—my thinking and my emotions—are so fouled up that I cannot distinguish the truth from a lie, then I cannot bear this fruit of the Spirit. If I am in turmoil on the inside, then my actions will probably betray my condition. What we need, then, is a way of ordering our inner lives so that they are under control. We need faithfulness.

The Faithfulness of God

Christians reflect faithfulness because their Lord is faithful. The Bible is a witness to a faithful God who does what He says He will do. Here are some of the things that God is faithful in doing.

God is faithful in establishing and keeping His covenants (agreements) with His people. Moses told the people who had come out of the Egyptian slavery: "Know therefore that the LORD your God is God; he is the faithful God, keeping his covenant of love to a thousand generations of those who love him and keep his commands" (Deut. 7:9). The writer of the book of Hebrews notes a similar promise. Referring to the Lord's promise to give salvation to those who trust Him, the writer says, "Let us hold unswervingly to the hope we profess, for he who promised is faithful" (Heb. 10:23).

God is faithful in calling people to Himself. Paul said, "God, who has called you into fellowship with his Son Jesus Christ our Lord, is faithful" (1 Cor. 1:9). The psalmist declared, "I will sing of the love of the LORD forever; with my mouth I will make your faithfulness known through all generations" (Ps. 89:1).

God is faithful in not allowing us to be crushed by the burdens we bear. Paul wrote, "No temptation has seized you except what is common to man. And God is faithful; he will not let you be tempted beyond what you can bear. But when you are tempted, he will also provide a way out so that you can stand up under it" (1 Cor. 10:13).

God is faithful in helping His people mature thoroughly. Paul said, "May God himself, the God of peace, sanctify you through and through. May your whole spirit, soul and body be kept blameless at the coming of our Lord Jesus Christ. The one who calls you is faithful and he will do it" (1 Thess. 5:23–24).

God is faithful in protecting his people from evil. Paul put it this way: "But the Lord is faithful, and he will strengthen and protect you from the evil one. We have confidence in the Lord that you are doing and will continue to do the things we command. May the Lord direct your hearts into God's love and Christ's perseverance" (2 Thess. 3:3–4).

God is faithful to His own truth. Paul asked, "What if some did not have faith? Will their lack of faith nullify God's faithfulness? Not at all! Let God be true, and every man a liar" (Rom. 3:3–4a). In writing to Timothy, Paul declared, "If we are faithless, he will remain faithful, for he cannot disown himself" (2 Tim. 2:13).

To all of this William Barclay notes, "With one voice the (biblical) writers witness to that which they themselves had over and over again experienced—the great truth that we can depend on God."[2] If God is faithful, trustworthy, and capable of being believed, it follows that those who claim to love Him should likewise be faithful. When a person commits his or her life to God through Christ, that commitment is something like a marriage vow. In fact, it is even better because it nowhere states, "Till death do us part." A commitment in faith says something like this: "Lord, I promise to give myself to you and to follow your leading in faith. I vow to be faithful to this calling every day of my life. Where I am weak, give me strength. Where I am ignorant, give me knowledge. Where I am arrogant, give me humility. Where I am disquieted, give me patience. Father, I give myself to you through your Son."

This is not easy to do, and I would not want to suggest otherwise. To commit yourself to God is a decision that changes your outlook, your perspective, your will, and your actions. You wind up in that strange tension between knowing God but at the same time always seeking to know Him more.

Even when times are tough, the knowledge of the trustworthiness of God carries us through. A Russian Baptist who spent time in a labor camp because of his faith expressed this fact in the following poem:

> Behind the bars of a murky prison
> Days and nights with prayer I meet.
> And in the presence of resentment
> And evil I feel the prayers of my friends.
> God gives me quiet sleep,
> Though the restless people don't sleep.
> And although the hours to me are unknown,
> During the night he awakens me twice,
> So that I'd hear him in the quiet,
> At three or four every night.
> Someone, somewhere from his whole heart
> For me before God is interceding.
> And tears run down my cheeks,
> And to God ascends a grateful prayer.
> I'm in prison often interrogated;
> Through the prayers of friends I'm strengthened.
> Do not carelessly waste your days,
> My dear friends, for you know yourselves
> In bonds, strength and power are seen,
> For a prison is a real exam.[3]

How strange it seems, at least on the surface, that in conditions almost unimaginably bad, this Christian knows of the faithfulness of God. And this is true not only of people in prison camps but also of people everywhere who turn to Him for support.

Flannery O'Connor, the late novelist from Georgia, was a devout Christian who never gave up her faith even though she had an incurable illness and died at a fairly early age. She once wrote to one of her readers, giving advice that I have found full of wisdom: "What people don't realize is how much religion costs. They think faith is a big electric blanket, when of course, it is the cross. It is much harder to believe than not to believe, you must at least do this: keep an open mind. Keep it open toward faith, keep wanting it, keep asking for it, and leave the rest to God."[4] She was right. To do this, we learn to be faithful to ourselves.

Staying Faithful to Oneself

God is faithful to do as He said He would. I do not doubt His veracity at all. My problem, and probably yours, too, comes with my own faithfulness. Like most Christians, I have deep-seated beliefs about certain matters. These beliefs include the nature of God, the work of the church, and other theological matters. They also include ideas about how I should act.

This is where I often fail because I am not consistent in my actions. I am not always loving toward people who dislike me, even though I believe I should be. I am not always generous toward people who try to use me for their own purposes, even though I know I should try to work with them. But this does not include allowing people to manipulate me. I am not even always kind to my own family, even though they are the most important people in the world to me.

My purpose for mentioning this is not to parade my weaknesses, although there is nothing wrong with confession. Instead, my purpose is to speak to the issue of faithfulness as it relates to the inner life. The saints of all ages have known the tension that exists for followers of Christ. They feel lead of God in one direction but feel pulled by many forces in another direction.

I know of no better statement of this dilemma than the one from Paul in Romans 7. Consider his statement: "We know that the law is spiritual; but I am unspiritual, sold as a slave to sin. I do not understand what I do. For what I want to do I do not do, but what I hate I do. And if I do what I do not want to do, I agree that the law is good. As it is, it is no longer I myself who do it, but it is sin living in me. I know that nothing good lives in me, that is, in my sinful nature. For I have the desire to do what is good, but I cannot carry it out. For what I do is not the good I want to do; no, the evil I do not want to do—this I keep on doing" (vv. 14–19).

After making this statement, Paul says, "What a wretched man I am! Who will rescue me from this body of death? Thanks be to God—through Jesus Christ our Lord!" (Rom. 7:24–25).

Most people with any sense of self-awareness can identify with Paul's situation. He says that he had a sinful nature and it contributed to his dilemma. This is true for you and me, too. But for a short time allow me to set aside a consideration of the nature of sin and plunge into the matter of faithfulness related to ourselves. I have a hunch about why Christians sometimes fail to live up to their potential. See if it makes sense to you. We often fail and blame the failure on sin, when in fact the failure is due simply to our not trying hard enough to avoid the behavior.

Let me be specific. I sometimes lose my patience with my children. I raise my voice and sometimes speak harshly to them. When this happens, I feel badly afterward. I could just shrug my shoulders and say, "Oh well, sin made me do this." But in fact nothing or nobody made me shout at my boys. I did it myself, and I have nothing or no one to blame but myself. I must therefore work hard to "keep a lid on" myself and not just go flying off the proverbial handle every time my children get a little loud. I believe strongly that children need room and time to grow, and they need parental permission to develop their own personalities. While I believe this, I do not always act in line with my belief. I must work to be faithful to my beliefs. And work it is!

The late theologian Dietrich Bonhoeffer noted that faithfulness and discipleship to Christ are similar. He suggested that for Christians to follow Christ, they must take up the cross daily. Bonhoeffer wrote, "To endure the cross is not a tragedy; it is the suffering which is the fruit of an exclusive allegiance to Jesus Christ. When it comes, it is not an accident, but a necessity. It is not the sort of suffering which is inseparable from this mortal life, but the suffering which is an essential part of the specifically Christian life."[5]

Faithfulness is necessary for any endeavor, religious or secular. Former president Calvin Coolidge noted that keeping to the task is essential. "Nothing in this world can take the place of persistence. Talent will not; nothing is more common than unsuccessful men with talent. Genius will not; unrewarded genius is almost a proverb. Education will not; the world is full of educated derelicts. Persistence and determination are alone omnipotent. The slogan 'press on' has solved and always will solve the problems of the human race."[6]

Faithfulness will enable us to do the right thing, regardless of the pressures on us. This takes strength and courage, especially when the stakes are high. But moral action takes place in the arena of the spirit.

Armstrong Williams spoke about this matter as follows:

> Most acts of courage will not be physical ones like those of a television action hero. Most courageous acts are moral ones. They aren't glamorous or often even appreciated, which make them all the more courageous. Moral courage entails resisting the little daily pressures and enticements of the world. It sometimes means taking an unpopular stand. It means subtle things like resisting peer pressure, or refusing to take the easy way out. It ultimately means facing up to your duties and obligations, taking responsibility for yourself and your actions, and what results from them. It means doing right even—especially—when it is not easy.[7]

Armstrong compares this necessary faithfulness and courage to the Old Testament prophets. They spoke out, no matter what. The results are there for us to read. He continues, "Courage and perseverance do not necessarily insure success in the worldly sense. Christ was despised and murdered by the world. But they are absolute prerequisites to real success in anything—success cannot be had without them. And courage gets results. It helps us make changes in ourselves and accomplish our higher duties. The results of acting with courage are what make life worth living."

Building a life worthy of the Christian calling is tough, but it is worth all of the effort. This is true in every area of life. A convicted murderer sat on death row in a Florida prison. He was a black man with seemingly very little going for him, but he found the forgiveness of God through his faith in Christ. He kept a journal of his days waiting for execution, and one entry reads as follows:

Monday, June 7, 7:05 P.M.

I wonder, what success have my classmates found? I know of those who found their graves with: needle in arm, bottle in hand, childbirth, police bullet.

America, America, in teeth of your brutality I have nonetheless been fond of living in this land. Yet I am merely "nigger," without history, a thing upon the auction block. I am tempted to hate you, but hatred is a sickness, my friend. Thus, before each of your hands pulls the switch, though terrified and powerless, I will echo, "I love you." Thus will I remain Doug.[8]

Doug found that, by refusing to hate the "system" and the people in it, he could be faithful to his inner conviction of love. Refusing to hate—that is the key! We say things like, "He makes me so angry!" but in fact no one can make you angry without your permission.

I am impressed with the way people in churches often seem to get their feelings hurt. I know of people who have dropped out of church because of some unintended or innocent remark made to them. Others stopped attending because they felt someone had slighted them in some way. I sometimes want to ask why we are such emotional infants who can be offended or hurt so easily. If someone does not speak to you at church, he might not be trying to avoid you or hurt you. He might be feeling an enormous load of inner conflict that has nothing to do with you. We would do very well to give others the benefit of our generosity in attitude. And think about this: Suppose that someone did intentionally offend you or say something unkind to or about you. Does it really matter? Can their attitude actually injure you? It cannot if you refuse to let it. Be faithful to your own inner convictions, and you will find that few perceived slights will bother you.[9]

The question naturally arises here, "How can I be faithful to myself?" One way is through what Lewis Smedes calls "the power of promising."[10] He says that this is the only way to overcome the unpredictability of the future: "If forgiving is the only remedy for your painful past, promising is the only remedy for your uncertain future."

Folk wisdom often says that we cannot do anything about the future, but the fact is that we *can* affect the future. By deciding now about certain matters, I can control how I will act in certain situations in the future. For example, when I got married, I promised Carla to be a faithful husband. There have been times during our marriage when I found other women trying to "come on" to me. I'm no "superman," but I refused to become involved with them because of a promise I had made years earlier. This also happens in so many other ways. Consider the following example.

Somewhere, perhaps close to you, is a woman who is the wife of an alcoholic. She wants to throw in the towel and is tempted when secular wisdom says, "Don't stay in a rough relationship—bail out at the earliest convenience." She has a desire to call an end to the problems of such a marriage. But she remembers the vows she made many years earlier—"for better or worse, in sickness and in health." These are her true convictions, so she does the best she can for herself and her children. She investigates organizations such as Al-Anon and Al-A-Teen, which offer help to families of alcoholics. The power of her promise keeps her steady personally even if it might not change the drinking habits of her husband. She is being faithful to herself.

Somewhere, perhaps close to you, is a man whose son is running wild. He is driving the father crazy, and the man is tempted to tell the boy to pack his bags and hit the road. But he remembers the vows he made years earlier at the infant dedication service at his church. He promised to raise the boy and do the very best for him, no matter what. So he decides to do what he can for the boy while he is still under the father's roof. He is being faithful to himself.

Somewhere, perhaps close to you, is a minister who has a first-class case of burnout. He is tired of encouraging other people who seem so ungrateful. He is sick to death of having to grind out two sermons each week for people who seem to care nothing for what he has to say. He is angry that the church has kept his salary frozen for several years, even though his education is comparable to the other executives and educators in the church. This minister wants to chuck the whole thing and go into some profession where he could make a decent living and feel that he contributes something to someone. But he thinks about his inner feeling of being called of God to be a minister. He remembers the vows he made years ago at his ordination service to serve wherever God calls him. So he renews his faith and takes a fresh look at the place of service he has now and goes on doing the best he can. He is being faithful to himself.

Three people—typical people really—who represent millions of people who have a tough time with certain situations in their lives. What keeps them going? Why should a woman stay with an alcoholic husband even though their relationship could have been the basis of Thomas Hardy's description of a marriage as "stale familiarity"? And the father of the wild son? Why not boot him out with the other million or so teenagers who run away from home or who are kicked out each year? Should he not have to lie in the bed he made? And what of the minister who feels so tired and disgusted? Why should he not seek some place else to go where there might be a little more money, or opportunity, or realization of his worth on the part of the people?

The "why not" in each of these examples is answered with one word—*faithfulness*. The apostle Paul knew more about hardship than I ever will, so he is certainly entitled to speak about it. He wrote to his young friend Timothy, "You then, my son, be strong in the grace that is in Christ Jesus. And the things you have heard me say in the presence of many witnesses entrust to reliable men who will also be qualified to teach others. Endure hardship with us like a good soldier of Christ Jesus" (2 Tim. 2:1–3).

Endure. This is an ominous sounding word, but without it faithfulness is impossible. This is true of any great undertaking. Edward Gibbon spent twenty years working on his monumental book *The Decline and Fall of the Roman Empire.* Noah Webster worked for thirty-six years on the dictionary that bears his name. George Bancroft sifted notes and researched for twenty-six years to produce his classic work *History of the United States.* The message is clear. If you want to produce anything worthwhile, especially a life, then remain faithful to your inner convictions.

Someone said in relation to faithfulness,

> One of the commonest mistakes and one of the costliest
> is thinking that success is due to some genius, some
> magic—something or other which we do not possess.
> Success is generally due to holding on, and failure to let-
> ting go. You decide to learn a language, study music, take
> a course of reading, train yourself physically. Will it be
> success or failure? It depends upon how much pluck and
> perseverance the word *decide* contains. The decision that
> nothing can overrule, the grip that nothing can detach
> will bring success. Remember the Chinese proverb, "With
> time and patience, the mulberry leaf becomes satin."[11]

Anything significant that is attained comes through hard work,
at least on the part of someone. Even the person who is given everything on the fabled "silver platter" must realize that someone
had to work hard for that money. The person who wants success
in his or her chosen field must be willing to put in the time and
effort to succeed. I have friends who want to write books, but they
are not willing to undertake the hard work of writing. Until they
do, they will dream of the "easy" life of the writer and imagine fat
royalty checks coming in. This is a dream, sure enough![12]

I am speaking here about being faithful to yourself, and this
includes working to fulfill your goals. But allow me to remind you
that life is not just hard work. The word *career* comes from the
French meaning "race course"; thus, a career can be just a rat race.
Being faithful to God, to others, and to yourself also includes well-
rounded and balanced living. This means that life is more than
constant work. Recreation is literally re-creation—of mind, body,
and spirit.

Faithfulness is a fruit of the Spirit that is a steadying influence
in shaky and uncertain times. As such, it is like a hand that holds
us in firm grip both to strengthen and to calm. Paul wrote to Timothy that "the Lord knows those who are his" (2 Tim. 2:19). It is
the faithfulness of His hand that holds us in firm grip even if we
struggle with Him. Not a bad deal, is it?

The great mind knows the power of gentleness.
                                    —Robert Browning

Chapter 8

A Powerful Weakness
GENTLENESS

WHAT DOES THE WORD *gentleness* suggest to you? Does it bring to mind a picture of Barney Fife? Does it make you think of a self-loathing person who will not look another person in the eye, and who sees himself as merely the doormat for others to walk on?

Many people seem to associate all of these images, and others equally repugnant, with the word *gentleness*. These impressions, however, have very little to do with the biblical meaning of gentleness.

In Galatians 5:22, in which Paul lists the fruit of the Spirit, gentleness does not suggest spinelessness and spiritlessness and a lack of strength and virility. Some older versions of the Bible use the word *meekness* here, but this is even more apt to be misunderstood than *gentleness*. The original word is *prautes,* but there seems to be no one English word that will carry over its full meaning. Whatever else it means, it does not suggest weakness or lack of courage. Gentleness is a power that seems at first glance like a weakness. But it is "the power through which by the help of the Spirit of God the strong and explosive might of the passions is harnessed in the service of men and of God."[1]

As part of the fruit of the Spirit, gentleness is a powerful weakness. It holds itself in subjection to reserve its energy to accomplish its goals. We might think of it this way. The difference between a river and a swamp has to do with the banks. A swamp has no clearly defined banks, so it oozes out all over. But a river, such as the Mississippi, has definite banks, which hold it in the channel. A river thus flows powerfully rather than oozing listlessly along. Gentleness is more like a river than a swamp. Its energy and power are harnessed for specific purposes.

Even so, many people have trouble thinking of themselves in terms of gentleness. This seems to be an undesired and unvalued quality. In Bud Blake's comic strip *Tiger,* a little boy stands and watches a girl carry a football past him. When his teammates criticize him for not tackling her, the boy says, "I was afraid I'd hurt her." The last frame of the strip shows this little boy walking home with head down and shoulders slumped, saying, "I got thrown out of the game for unnecessary gentleness."[2]

Who cannot identify with his dilemma? The church preaches meekness—gentleness, humility, "softness"—take your pick of synonyms here—but almost no one else values it. Sheldon Vanauken went to Oxford University for graduate study. At that time, he was not a Christian, but he began investigating its claims. He also began writing to C. S. Lewis about the claims of faith. In one of his letters to Lewis, Vanauken confessed that of all the elements of faith, humility (or gentleness) seemed on the surface the most repugnant. He wrote, "Indeed, there is nothing in Christianity which is so repugnant to me as humility—the bent knee. If I knew beyond hope or despair that Christianity were true, my fight for ever would have to be against the pride of 'the spine may break but it never bends.'"[3]

I think I understand why this man was so repulsed by the idea of humility. It was because he had a popular—and mistaken—view of what the Bible means by humility, or gentleness. To be gentle does not mean to be inactive or docile. When I lose myself in Christ, I do not simply cease to exist, but rather I emerge, having found myself in a new way. As Jesus put it, "Whoever finds his life will lose it, and whoever loses his life for my sake will find it." Vanauken, and many others like him, understood the first half of

Jesus' statement, but not the second half. I find my life when I so intertwine my life with Christ that I am no longer myself alone. Whatever else this might be, it is not boring!

Understanding Gentleness

The Bible has a cluster of words that convey a meaning similar to "gentleness." These words include *lowliness, meekness, patience,* and *forbearance.* All of these words, along with *gentleness,* signify someone who is so strong that he need not prove his strength.

For example, Jesus is described this way. He said, "Take my yoke upon me and learn from me, for I am gentle and humble in heart, and you will find rest for your souls" (Matt. 11:29). But his gentleness was no weakness. No one but an incredibly strong person could have lived with the abuse and misunderstanding that Jesus suffered—not to mention the worst abuse, the cross. He voluntarily surrendered his status as sovereign Lord to become one with us, to walk where we walk, to identify with us, and to suffer for us (see Phil. 2:5–11). He was much too concerned about the welfare of others to spend his time and energy defending himself all the time. He had other work to do.

When I was in the seventh grade, a group of us were playing baseball at recess. The largest and strongest boy in our class was named Cecil. One of the smallest boys was named Jerry. During one play, Cecil was playing second base and Jerry was trying to run from first to second. As Jerry came flying into second, he slammed into Cecil and fell down. He jumped up and pushed Cecil, yelling, "Hey, watch it, boy!" All of us on the field held our breath as we imagined what Cecil was about to do to Jerry. I could almost see him pound little Jerry into the dust. Instead, Cecil just smiled and said, "Yes, sir," and walked back to his base to resume play. The rest of us boys talked about that for a long time, and I remember it vividly these many years later. Cecil displayed on the baseball field an attitude that was close to what the New Testament calls gentleness. He could have really hurt Jerry, but what was the point? Everyone already knew he was stronger.

Malcolm Tolbert spoke about this matter thus: "People who are secure in their own persons and in their relationship with God do not lord it over their brothers and sisters. Persons secure in this way identify with others and share their weaknesses and their needs. People marked by lowliness or humility do not think about personal glory but about the welfare of those whom Christ loves."[4]

Thus, gentleness and strength go together. If you consider it, you will probably realize that the people you know who have the most inner strength are some of the most humble and gentle people anywhere. I know a man who has a black belt in karate, but you would never guess it by looking at him. He does not strut around like a bantam rooster, trying to prove something. This friend is aware that he is well capable of defending himself if someone ever tried to hurt him, but he does not go out of his way to show off. Centuries ago, the philosopher Plato realized that gentleness and strength go together. Plato spoke of a watchdog who is bravely hostile to strangers and gently friendly with people he knows and trusts.

The Bible speaks with one voice in its condemnation of aggressive, arrogant pride, which is the opposite of gentleness. Job says that the Lord will vindicate the justice of the gentle whereas the arrogant and prideful person will suffer (Job 36:15). The Psalms are replete with such references. Consider the following verses: "The Lord sustains the humble but casts the wicked to the ground" (147:6). "Have mercy on us, O Lord, have mercy on us, for we have endured much contempt. We have endured much ridicule from the proud, much contempt from the arrogant" (123:3–4). "Good and upright is the Lord; therefore he instructs sinners in his ways. He guides the humble in what is right and teaches them his way" (25:8–9).

Many people have memorized Proverbs 3:5–6: "Trust in the Lord with all your heart and lean not on your own understanding; in all your ways acknowledge him, and he will make your paths straight." This council helps us to realize that only by acknowledging our weaknesses can we hope to overcome them. As someone put it, "True humility isn't saying that we're dumb and that we can't do anything right, it's knowing our own weaknesses and struggles, and honestly admitting them. Standing before the Lord God Almighty, our best strengths are nothing compared to His awesome power and wisdom."[5]

Learning Personal Gentleness

Have you ever noticed how different people can be? Some seem calm and serene on both the inside and the outside. They seem to take life in stride and never get ruffled. For these people, being gentle with others is not something at which they have to work hard. It comes easily and naturally. Other people are just the opposite. They act as if they have just finished their fifteenth cup of coffee and the caffeine is getting to them. They seem jittery and get upset at the least annoyance. For these folks to display gentleness takes great effort and concentration. These individual differences among people are evident to anyone who will look for them. The point is that while some people have an easier time with this fruit of the Spirit, most of us have to learn how to cultivate it.

William Barclay says that gentleness in the New Testament conveys three main ideas: submission to the will of God, teachableness, and consideration of others.[6] The first two of these ideas are similar. For one to be submissive to the will of God, he or she must be open to God's instruction. As Paul put it in Ephesians 5:17, "Therefore do not be foolish, but understand what the Lord's will is." Again, some people find it easier to do this than others. The plain fact is that some people refuse even to consider anything new or beyond their own current understanding. A well-known educator used to say that in his work he found three types of ignorance: simple ignorance, don't-know-and-don't-care ignorance, and just plain cussed ignorance!

Learning gentleness is first of all learning about God in a personal relationship. It is opening yourself to learn and experience thoughts, feelings, and willpower that you may have never known before. To do this removes you from the narrow-minded precepts of those who think they have it made and need nothing else. The Lord delivered His judgment on such people through His spokesman Jeremiah: "This is what the LORD says: 'Cursed is the one who trusts in man, who depends on flesh for his strength and whose heart turns away from the LORD'" (17:5). His promise is given through Isaiah: "For this is what the high and lofty One says—he who lives forever, whose name is holy: 'I live in a high and holy place, but also with him who is contrite and lowly in spirit, to revive the spirit of the lowly and to revive the heart of the contrite'" (57:15).

To be gentle is to allow your total self—mind, body, and spirit—to be at the disposal of God. It is to stop rebelling and bucking so that all of your energy can be harnessed for something useful. When you do this, you discover that your trust in God increases because of what He is able to do with and through you. Jeremiah wrote, "This is what the LORD says: 'Let not the wise man boast of his wisdom or the strong man boast of his strength or the rich man boast of his riches, but let him who boasts boast about this: that he understands and knows me, that I am the LORD, who exercises kindness, justice and righteousness on earth, for in these I delight,' declares the LORD" (9:23–24).

Paul understood this principle, too. He had all the right credentials for bragging about achievements on a worldly basis. But Paul realized that something was more important than personal achievement. That something is a personal relationship with God through Christ. He had a physical problem, which he called his "thorn in the flesh," and he asked God to remove it. This was the answer Paul got: "But he said to me, 'My grace is sufficient for you, for my power is made perfect in weakness.' Therefore I will boast all the more gladly about my weaknesses, so that Christ's power may rest on me. That is why, for Christ's sake, I delight in weaknesses, in insults, in hardships, in persecutions, in difficulties. For when I am weak, then I am strong" (2 Cor. 12:9–10). Some people might see Paul's gentleness as weakness, but in God's eyes, it is a powerful weakness.

One of the early church fathers was Thomas à Kempis. He realized that by admitting our weaknesses we learn to be loving and gentle, both with ourselves and others. He wrote, "For nothing can humble us and confound us before God more than a sense of our own miseries, and nothing can be more just than that we should bear in others those things which we would have them support in ourselves. We should, therefore, bear with the tempers of others and endeavor to give no cause of uneasiness to anyone on account of our own. It is thus, according to St. Paul, we shall carry one another's burdens and fulfill the law of Jesus Christ, which is a law of charity, meekness and patience."[7]

As we strive to learn the lesson of gentleness, we should remember to be gentle with ourselves and not to get frustrated when it does not come quickly or easily. Francis de Sales, who lived in France from 1567 until 1622, wrote a book, *Introduction to the Devout Life,* which has become a classic of devotional literature. In this work, he realized how easily Christians can get discouraged in their efforts to grow in faith and virtue and wrote,

> One of the best exercises of meekness we can perform is that of . . . never fretting at our own imperfections; for though reason requires that we should be sorry when we commit any fault, yet we must refrain from that bitter, gloomy, spiteful, and passionate displeasure for which we are greatly to blame, who, being overcome by anger, are angry for having been angry and vexed to see ourselves; for by this means we keep our hearts perpetually steeped in passion; and though it seems as if the second anger destroyed the first, it serves, nevertheless, to open a passage for fresh anger on the first occasion that shall present itself. Besides, this anger and vexation against ourselves tend to pride, and flow from no other source than self-love, which is troubled and disquieted to see itself imperfection.
>
> We must be displeased at our faults, but in a peaceable, settled, and firm manner; for, as a judge punishes malefactors much more justly when he is guided in his decisions by reason, and proceeds with the spirit of tranquillity than when he acts with violence and passion (because judging in his passion, he does not punish the faults according to their enormity, but according to his passion), so we correct ourselves much better by a calm and steady repentance than by that which is harsh, turbulent, and passionate; for repentance exercised with violence proceeds not according to the quality of our faults but according to our inclinations.[8]

Part of this gentleness is to be shown toward the faults of others, too. Jesus had no kind word for those who could find a speck in their brother's eye but who overlooked the two-by-four in their own eye. On the contrary, he continually preached the gospel of love and peace, which surely includes consideration. You cannot win another person to your viewpoint or your faith by intimidating him or her. You must attract that person with loving-kindness.

Paul knew of this truth and referred to it when writing to his young friend Timothy: "And the Lord's servant must not quarrel; instead, he must be kind to everyone, able to teach, not resentful. Those who oppose him he must gently instruct, in the hope that God will grant them repentance leading them to a knowledge of the truth, and that they will come to their senses and escape from the trap of the devil, who has taken them captive to do his will" (2 Tim. 2:24–26).

I am not sure why, but religion seems to make some people meaner instead of nicer! When a man thinks that he has God in his hip pocket, that he has all the answers, and that if you do not see things his way you are obviously wrong and controlled by the Devil, then there is little hope of such a person winning another through gentle instruction and correction. Some people just will not admit to being wrong or to not knowing something, and will argue and defend their positions even if those positions are ill informed and absurd.

Dr. Samuel Johnson was an English writer who published his *Dictionary of the English Language* in 1755. He was a brilliant man with encyclopedic knowledge and a sharp wit. Yet Johnson would argue with anyone on just about every subject and never back down. One of the men who knew him well said of him, "The most light and airy dispute was with him a dispute in the arena. He fought on every occasion as if his whole reputation depended upon the victory of the minute, and he fought with all his weapons. If he was foiled in argument, he had recourse to abuse and rudeness." Another person said of him, "There is no arguing with Johnson; for, when his pistol misses fire, he knocks you down with the butt end of it." Still another friend wrote, "There is no disputing with him. He will not hear you, and, having a louder voice that you, must roar you down."[9]

The point of this discussion is to stress the need for intellectual and emotional openness toward others and toward God as we learn to live with gentleness. One reason why we have so much trouble with this aspect of spiritual life is that not much in our culture prepares us for it. We are not taught to be gentle but rather to be aggressive and competitive. From the time children are in the first grade, and sometimes earlier, they are put in classes with other youngsters and taught how to compete for grades and position within the class. Some people learn competition so well that they cannot function normally without it. One man I know of was a brilliant student. He went through college and then graduate school making the top grades. When he finished his Ph.D. degree, he underwent a long period of depression. He had no more academic mountains to climb. He had reached the top and had no one else with whom to compete. He could not stand it!

A friend of mine once gave me a book entitled *Rhinoceros Success*. She signed the book, "To Don, from one Rhino to Another." This book is about how to act like a rhinoceros in the sense of being aggressive, charging, never letting up. The author says, "The secret of success is, naturally, becoming a rhinoceros. In fact, my wish for you is that you wake up tomorrow morning as a full-grown, six-thousand-pound rhinoceros!"[10] These creatures of the jungle charge madly, have a thick skin that no criticism can penetrate, and, in general, scare the heck out of the competition.

I told my friend that I appreciated the book, as I always do with the gifts of friends, but I wondered why she thought of me as a rhino. She explained that it is because I never give up, I know what I want to accomplish and take criticism in stride—all supposedly like a rhino. I mention this book because many people feel the way that author does. They are out to make a name, to accomplish something great, to earn a large paycheck. Always charging and never backing off, many of these people have never learned that even rhinos enjoy just lying in the mud sometimes. Another of my friends, while under forty, vowed to be a millionaire by the time he was fifty. He drove himself mercilessly and experienced great conflicts at home and in his work. To paraphrase an old proverb, All aggression and no gentleness makes Jack a very dull boy.

Sports in America seem to feed what has been called the "killer instinct." Lately this instinct has married Christian teaching, and the offspring has been some theological freak. Former boxer Floyd

Patterson credited God for helping him knock out Archie Moore to win his heavyweight championship a few years ago. Patterson said, "I could see his eyes go glassy as he fell back, and I knew if he got up again it wouldn't do him any good. I just hit him and the Lord did the rest."[11]

Really? Did the great Lord of the universe care anything about two men trying to knock each other's heads off? Did the One who gave Himself in Christ and who went to the cross to prove His love really "do the rest" when Patterson hit his opponent? I really doubt it!

We have gotten so caught up in the sanctification of sports that we seem unable to think straight any more. I admire the honesty of Doug Plank, a former defensive back for the Chicago Bears, who realized that his athletic and religious lives were often in conflict. Plank said, "As a Christian, I learn to love, but when the whistle blows I have to be tough. You're always on a tightrope." At least he realized his dilemma. I have read the New Testament through many times, and I never recall finding one verse that says anything like, "You shall love your neighbor as yourself, except when he is your opponent in an athletic match, at which time you have complete liberty to pulverize him."

What, then, are we to think about aggression in sports and Christian faith? The late basketball great "Pistol" Pete Maravich learned fairly late in his life that there is much more to life than winning on the basketball court. When he signed a $1.5 million contract with the Atlanta Hawks, Maravich was at that time the highest paid rookie in the history of the NBA. He worked hard in his playing, was traded several times, and ended his career in 1980 after playing for the Boston Celtics for one year.

Maravich's life was strange, by his own account. He learned karate from a master, so he had the ability to kill. He became a Hindu and believed in reincarnation. He then became a believer of UFOism. Still later, he tried yoga, survivalism, vegetarianism, and began drinking a lot. In all of this, he was groping for some meaning in his life beyond the basketball court. Then, in 1982, he had an encounter with Christ. He said, "I woke in the middle of the night in a cold sweat and heard the Lord tell me to be strong in the heart. I was immediately a changed person."[12] He went on, "I found out that there are things more important than basketball. Jesus is the answer. I am now dedicating my life to the Lord and am going out to tell about his great works."

The point of all this discussion is to speak to the issue of gentleness and to note how this element of spiritual living is often at odds with many of the prevailing philosophies around us. This includes not only sports but also business. I heard of a man with a sign in his office that reads, "If the meek inherit the earth, then what will happen to us tigers?"

The New Testament nowhere asks people to roll over and play dead. That is not gentleness; that is laziness. What the New Testament does is help us retool our thinking and emotions and put our inner lives in order. Thus, we can live in this grace-filled manner that is called gentleness. Whether we make giant impacts upon the world is hardly the point. As Charles Kingsley put it, "We are surely not sent into the world to get credit and reputations, but to speak such words as are given us to do; not heeding much, nor expecting to know whether they have effected anything or nothing. Therefore friends, be of good courage."[13]

St. Teresa lived from 1515 until 1582. She headed up a group of nuns and wrote spiritual books and tracts to help them live gentle lives in Christ. In one of her works, Teresa offered the following advice to the self-important: "It is very important for us to realize that God does not lead us all by the same road. . . . Remember that there must be someone to cook the meals and count yourselves happy in being able to serve like Martha. Reflect that true humility consists to a great extent in being ready for what the Lord desires to do with you. Remember that the Lord walks among the pots and pans and that He will help you in the inward tasks and in the outward too."[14]

The world seems full of "important" people who push and shove and scramble for the top. Christ emerges from the pages of the New Testament as our eternal contemporary who urges us to do our best but never to seek the places of honor. He bids us come and die with Him, and in so doing, we will find authentic life. His gentleness inspires us to imitate Him.

Truly, gentleness is the most powerful of weaknesses.

*If you would learn self-mastery, begin by yielding
yourself to the One Great Master.*
—Johann Friedrich Lobstein

Chapter 9

Stifle Yourself!

S E L F - C O N T R O L

THE OLD TELEVISION PROGRAM *All in the Family,* now seen in syndication, featured Archie and Edith Bunker as the main characters. Archie was a loud, opinionated, and obnoxious bigot. Edith was a rather quiet, gentle soul who usually gave in to her husband's overbearing demands. One of the most obnoxious things Archie would say to Edith was "Edit', stifle yourself!" This became his stock reply many times when she would say something he did not want to hear.

The word *stifle* has a nerve-jarring sound to it. It comes from the old French *estouffer,* which means to smother or choke. One dictionary defines it thus: "To kill by preventing respiration; smother or suffocate."

What does all this have to do with the fruit of the Spirit? Some people seem to think that the last item in the list—self-control—is similar to Archie's demand of Edith. Some people I know have an image of God sitting on a throne in heaven saying to human beings, "Hey, you down there. Stifle yourself!" However, when Paul listed self-control among the fruit of the Spirit, he had no such thing in mind. His concept was not harsh and strident but was given for the well-being of those who learn to control themselves.

Understanding Self-Control

In centuries gone by, the church sometimes thought of self-control in terms of severe discipline. Four general uses for this term were given by the church.[1] Discipline sometimes meant conduct that was governed by various rules and regulations. Second, discipline referred to forms of asceticism and mortification, such as self-beatings and living in monasteries. Third, it came to refer to a scourge, a whip of knotted cords, used to enforce discipline. Last, it was a way of life prescribed by the church and enforced on practitioners. For example, when the Reformation leader John Calvin lived in Geneva, he used his position to enforce severe discipline on the inhabitants of that city. It did not work for long, and Calvin was forced to flee Geneva.

The point of this is that some of our spiritual ancestors misunderstood what Paul meant by "self-control." Think of all of the other elements of the fruit of the Spirit. Are any of them harsh or ugly? Love, joy, peace, patience, kindness, goodness, faithfulness, gentleness—these are all positive and healthy values. This is true with self-control, too. It refers to a simple fact of life: You and I cannot have everything, do everything, or experience everything. We are limited in our time, our finances, and our ability to respond to various experiences. To be self-controlled is to acknowledge that not everything is good for you; therefore, it is to choose wisely and carefully among life's smorgasbord.

Paul wrote to Timothy, "For God did not give us a spirit of timidity, but a spirit of power, of love and of self-discipline" (2 Tim. 1:7). Paul referred here to a reasoned, well-ordered life. Discipline, self-discipline, and self-control are all similar concepts in the New Testament. None refers to a life lived in isolation from Christ, but they all put the responsibility for how we live squarely on our shoulders.

Here is one of the great paradoxes of our faith. On the one hand, we live in the Spirit. We are under His influence and guidance. As Paul wrote in Galatians 2:20, "I have been crucified with Christ and I no longer live, but Christ lives in me. The life I live in the body, I live by faith in the Son of God, who loved me and gave himself for me." On the other hand, we actually live. We are not dead, nor are we zombies. Ultimately, we have to take responsibility for our lives. We cannot blame God for our failures. As James put it, "When tempted, no one should say, 'God is tempting me.' For God cannot be tempted by evil, nor does he tempt anyone; but each one is tempted when, by his own evil desire, he is dragged away and enticed" (1:13–14). To mature in faith is to learn to trust God and to live the best we can but always to be responsible for our actions.

Fred Craddock once said that there is no way to modulate the human voice to make a whine acceptable to God. I think what he means is that we waste our time and God's when we try to evade responsibility for what we are and what we do. It is much better to say with Paul, "By the grace of God, I am what I am" (1 Cor. 15:10). In my opinion, people who refuse to take responsibility for themselves and who try to blame God for their mistakes and problems are just "spiritual brats."

Putting Self-Control into Practice

To be self-controlled does not mean, of course, that I do whatever I want without a thought of God or the welfare of others. This part of the fruit of the Spirit is not a license to be irresponsible. Too many times people have sought to be completely self-controlled in the sense of being self-centered. This if far from what Paul had in mind. William Ernest Henley wrote in his poem "Invictus,"

> I am the master of my fate,
> I am the captain of my soul.

Really? I think no man can be master of himself until he acknowledges Christ as his ultimate Master. Morgan Phelps Noyes thought about the sentiment expressed in Henley's poem and wrote, "No man is the master of his fate so long as he lives in a universe which he did not create, and no man is the captain of his soul so long as there are within him dark forces which need to be redeemed."[2]

Noyes is right on target. You and I are not totally free. We are influenced by impulses and forces both within and outside of ourselves. We need to be aware of and sensitive to these influences and not let them control our lives.

Too many people seem to wander around aimlessly, without any sense of inner purpose or goals. They drift from one fad to the next, from one lover to the next, from one job to the next, without really knowing what they want or how to achieve it. Abraham Heschel has noted, "Unfree men are horrified by the suggestion of accepting a daily discipline. Confusing inner control with external tyranny, they prefer caprice to self-restraint. They would rather have ideals than norms, hopes than directions, faith than forms. But the goal and the way cannot long endure in separation."[3]

Freedom comes from self-control. That seems strange, doesn't it? We intentionally limit ourselves in some matters and then find freedom. The fruit of the Spirit, especially self-control, takes life out of the realm of chance or the impulse of the moment. It puts us on the level of the long-range view. This is actually a theological issue. If life has no ultimate meaning and if God does not exist, then I am perfectly free simply to follow every impulse or desire I might have. As Paul put it when quoting pagan philosophy, "Let us eat and drink, for tomorrow we die" (1 Cor. 15:33). I could eat anything and everything because health would be irrelevant. I could become sexually involved with other women because faithfulness to my wife would have no meaning. I would not be concerned with working hard and doing my best because such standards would be absurd. All of this would be true if God did not exist and if life had no meaning.

But I believe that God lives and that life somehow makes sense. Therefore, I am enabled to take a long-range view of life. I do not eat anything and everything because not everything is good for me, and I do not want to get overweight and develop high blood pressure. I do not allow my normal and natural sexual desires to control me because I value my exclusive relationship with my wife much more than the fleeting pleasures of promiscuity. I try to work hard and do my best because I believe that what I do is important to others as well as to myself.

Self-control, then, is a holistic way of looking at life. It begins with a personal relationship with God through faith in Christ. It moves to the level of a disciplined mind. I am not referring primarily to trying to suppress certain thoughts. What I have in mind is the fact that the human mind does not operate well in neutral. It always is thinking, evaluating, planning, hoping. The key to disciplining the mind is not simply to remove certain thoughts, but rather to replace them with better thoughts and insight. Evelyn and John Whitehead have noted, "At the heart of Christian spirituality is the discipline of self-knowledge. This Christian self-knowledge includes freedom from both blind passion and social pressures; it seeks an awareness of God's gracious presence in my life. It is a strength that can be expected to characterize the mature Christian."[4]

A *Frank & Ernest* cartoon has the men looking at a book one of them is holding. Its title is *"No" Thyself.* Frank explains, "It's about self-control."[5] That is a great image. We learn to say "no" to some things so we can say "yes" to others. For the Christian, we learn to say "yes" to love. A mature life of self-control is characterized by love. In fact, Dr. Larry Crabb, a Christian psychologist, says that love is the very thing that points to a life that is graced by the Spirit. He wrote:

> The real proof of self-control, is that I'm willing to control whatever within me interferes with the expression of love, whatever interferes with movement toward people on their behalf. The disciplined Christian—the one who never misses devotions, who goes through his prayer list for an hour each day—is not necessarily exhibiting the fruit of the Spirit. You can be organized and be Spirit-filled.[6]

Crabb has nothing against self-discipline. He simply points out that self-control is part of the fruit of the Spirit that helps us love, no matter what gets in the way. He concludes, "Genuine self-control will develop only as we understand where life is: in loving God and loving others."

Sometimes we need to control our actions to be available for others. In an earlier chapter, we considered goodness. Goodness flows out of a life that is self-controlled through the Spirit. As John Erskine said, "Though we sometimes speak of a primrose path, we all know that a bad life is just as difficult, just as full of work, obstacles and hardships, as a good one. The only choice is the kind of life one would care to spend one's efforts on."[7] He is right, of course. Since a bad life is just as difficult—and I really think *more* difficult—why not spend our time and energy on something of worth and value?

Often, we need self-discipline that moves us toward self-control. This means that we have to learn to break out of the web of habits. Psychologist Denis Waitley said of this:

> Habits start out as off-hand remarks, magazine advertise-ments, friendly hints, experiments—like flimsy cobwebs with little substance. They grow with practice, layer upon layer—thought upon thought—fused with imagination and emotion until they become like steel cables—unbreakable. Habits are attitudes which grow from cobwebs into cables that control your everyday life. Self-discipline alone can make or break a habit. Self-discipline alone can effect a permanent change in your self-image and in you. Self-discipline achieves goals. Many people define self-discipline as "doing without." A better definition for discipline is "doing within." Self-discipline is mental practice—the commitment to memory of those thoughts and emotions that will override current information stored in the subconscious memory bank.[8]

Waitley is right. Self-control is not just stopping myself from doing something, but, more positively, helping myself to do something better. It begins with a disciplined imagination that allows me to "see" something better and therefore to reach out for it. The Christian need not fear the imagination because, like every other aspect of human life, it has enormous power for moral good as well as for evil. The fact is that we all have an imagination, re-gardless of whether we do anything with it. Why not put it to dis-ciplined use in service for Christ?

One of the most influential Christian leaders during the first third of this century was a man named S. Parkes Cadman. He wrote two books on the subject of imagination and its relationship to spiritual life. In one of these books Cadman noted, "Man as the self-conscious animal is the saddest spectacle extant; whereas man as the convinced son of God is the noblest. Why reflect hypochondria, diseased notions, or loathsome dreams when the strength and beauty of an orderly imagination, submissive to the things of the spirit, is at our command?"[9]

How easy it is to allow ourselves to drift along rather than to take command of our lives! Denis Waitley said, "I didn't realize until I was thirty-five that I'm behind the wheel in [my] life. I thought it was the government, inflation, and my heritage. I used to think that as a Gemini, I was destined to be creative, but non-specific."[10]

Think about it. Who, or what, controls your life? Do you read the horoscope each morning to see what you can or cannot do that day? Do you ask permission of your spouse, or your children, or your parents before you do anything? Do you brood regularly on how "they"—whomever "they" might be—are in your way, or block your happiness, or interfere with your life? One way of gaining some sense of self-control is to specify exactly what and who seem to be blocking your potential for creative living. Then the next step is to brainstorm ways of going around or through that blockage. I do not mean by this that you suddenly begin ignoring your family or telling your employer to jump in the lake. What I mean is that you try to get some objective perspective on your life. None of us can live in absolute and total control of our lives. We are born to parents whom we did not choose, live lives that are influenced by thousands of outside factors, and die at times over which we have little control. Every birth certificate comes with an expiration date! The key is not to let others steal your life.

Self-control also has to do with our emotional lives. If our emotions are severely damaged, we can get help through trained medical and mental-health professionals. One positive thing that has happened in recent years is that the stigma of mental problems has begun to fade. People who seek help for emotional and mental problems are no longer labeled as "crazy." The human mind is a delicate and finely tuned organ, and it can get out of balance fairly easily. I have seen troubled people virtually remade through the help of caring mental-health specialists. If your emotional or intellectual life seems beyond your control, please realize that there is no shame in seeking help.

People sometimes say things such as, "He makes me so mad!" and then they fly off into uncontrolled rage. I sometimes think of this as an emotional "meltdown." Self-control, as part of the fruit of the Spirit of God, helps us avoid these outbursts.

In the Old Testament, for example, Gideon gathered the various tribes of Israel and went into battle. But the tribe of the Ephraimites somehow got left out, and after the battle they responded: "Now the Ephraimites asked Gideon, 'Why have you treated us like this? Why didn't you call us when you went to fight Midian?' And they criticized him sharply. But he answered them, 'What have I accomplished compared to you? Aren't the gleanings of Ephraim's grapes better than the full grape harvest of Abiezer? God gave Oreb and Zeeb, the Midianite leaders, into your hands. What was I able to do compared to you?' At this, their resentment against him subsided" (Judg. 8:1–3).

Gideon's self-control accomplished everything he wanted, including easing the anger of his fellow countrymen, and he also maintained his leadership. Phillips Elliott commented on Gideon's self-control in this situation and went on to make an application to Christian faith. "If one wants to find the clearest test of greatness, can he do better than observing a man's humility? The proud man is the little man. The humble man is the big man. Wherever true humility resides, even though without secular acclaim, the marks of greatness can be seen. It is uniquely the mark of the Christian."[11]

To be a Christian does not mean that we are emotionless or listless. Far from it! It means, instead, that all of the emotional and mental energy we possess is channeled into constructive activities and purposes. Horse trainers know that very little can be done with a wild horse. It may possess tremendous strength, but that strength means little until the horse is broken and all that energy is focused in some specific direction. A horse that has been broken is no less powerful than an unbroken horse. The difference is that its power and energy are pooled together and focused into some set task, such as racing.

This is true of people, too. The difference between an athlete and a nonathlete may not be physical strength. The fellow who drinks a case of beer each day and does nothing more strenuous than watch football on TV may be just as strong as the man who earns his living on the gridiron. The difference is that the athlete has the self-discipline and self-control to keep himself in top shape and to focus his strength in one direction. I mentioned in the previous chapter the difference between a river and a swamp. That difference is applicable here, too. The TV watcher is like the swamp, and the disciplined athlete is like the river.

John Davies writes about self-control, "It includes the courage and wisdom to make my own judgments, neither in infantile enslavement to authority nor in adolescent rejection of authority: the maturity to take responsibility for my own belief and conscience, and not to hand over such responsibility to any political or religious or cultural authority. . . ." Also, "the ability to hear and care for the other person without being dominated by my own anxieties: a care for the wholeness and usefulness of my reason and my central nervous system and the whole bundle of faculties by which people can help each other. . . ." Davies concludes, "In short, this fruit of the spirit is a gift of self-government, autonomy, independence."[12]

Proverbs 16:32 makes an astounding affirmation: "Better a patient man than a warrior, a man who controls his temper than one who takes a city." Think of that. Keeping control over your temper is more important, and perhaps harder, than being a victor in battle.

Other proverbs support this claim: 14:29 says, "A patient man has great understanding, but a quick-tempered man displays folly"; 19:11 notes, "A man's wisdom gives him patience; it is to his glory to overlook an offense"; and 29:11 says, "A fool gives vent to his anger, but a wise man keeps himself under control."

Rolland Schloerb was right on target when he offered the following comment on these proverbs.

In fact, self-control might be considered the highest kind of power. A man may find himself in a position where he can exercise power over other people, but if he has not learned how to control himself, his power may bring disaster. "He who rules his spirit" is better "than he who takes a city." Having taken a city, the man without self-restraint may bring it to ruin by some foolish outburst of temper. He can hardly be trusted to rule over others because he has not learned how to rule himself. The wise man can direct his feelings of indignation into constructive channels. The person who has fits of temper is not necessarily more indignant than another person. The other person may control twice as much feeling but direct it like the explosions in the cylinders of a gasoline motor.[13]

Finding the Will Power for Self-Control

The biblical concept of self-control is not a "bootstrap" philosophy by which we simply make up our minds to be better and thereby solve all of our problems. The Bible is the most realistic book ever written. While some popular psychology seems to suggest that people can will their problems away, most psychologists are realistic enough to comprehend the depths of our human dilemma. Carl G. Jung, the well-known pioneer in psychological studies, wrote, "We are unable, for example, to suppress many of our emotions; we cannot change a bad mood into a good mood, and we cannot command our dreams to come or go. We only believe that we are masters in our own house because we like to flatter ourselves."[14]

To develop self-control, we have to find the willpower. We have to desire this aspect of spiritual living so much that we are willing to work and sweat and make sacrifices to make progress. One way to find this will power is to consider the lives of people who have exercised self-control and then to visualize yourself doing something similar. Look, for example, at the life of Booker T. Washington as recounted in his autobiography, *Up from Slavery*. Washington, born a slave but freed after The American Civil War, tells how he hungered for an education and how he was willing to do whatever it took to get it. This remarkable man remembered his days on the plantation and recalled that the system of slavery bred a spirit of laziness and a lack of discipline in many of the slave owners.

> The slave system on our place, in a large measure, took the spirit of self-reliance and self-help out of the white people. My old master had many boys and girls, but not one, so far as I know, ever mastered a single trade or special line of productive industry. The girls were not taught to cook, sew or to take care of the house. All this was left to the slaves. The slaves, of course, had little personal interest in the life of the plantation, and their ignorance prevented them from learning how to do things in the most improved and thorough manner. As a result of the system, fences were out of repair, gates were hanging half off the hinges, doors creaked, windowpanes were out, plastering had fallen but was not replaced, weeds grew in the yard. As a rule, there was food for whites and blacks, but inside the house, and on the dining-room table, there was wanting that delicacy and refinement of touch and finish which can make a home the most convenient, comfortable, and attractive place in the world. Withal there was a waste of food and other materials which was sad. When freedom came, the slaves were almost as well fitted to begin life anew as the master, except in the matter of book-learning and ownership of property. The slave owner and his sons had mastered no special industry. They unconsciously had imbibed the feeling that manual labour was not the proper thing for them. On the other hand, the slaves, in many cases, had mastered some handicraft, and none were ashamed, and few unwilling, to labour.[15]

Former slave owners who lacked the strength of self-discipline and self-control found themselves in a terrible dilemma when they were deprived of their workers. The lesson here for us is that we cannot depend on others to do everything for us. We must take care of ourselves. When I consider Washington's plight and what

Self-Discipline (( ))

he went through to get an education and do everything he could for himself, I am inspired to do my own best. Part of self-control is the determination to do what I can for myself.

Consider also the life of Glenn Cunningham. One cold February morning in 1916, Glenn, who was seven, and his older brother, Floyd, went into their school room to start a fire in the potbellied stove to warm the building before the other students arrived. Floyd poured what he thought was kerosene on what seemed to be cold wood. When he did, it exploded and burned him and Glenn badly. Later, they learned that a community club had met in the school the night before and used the stove. The fire had not died out when the boys arrived the next morning. Also, someone had put gasoline in the kerosene can.

The doctor came and examined both boys and told the family that, if infection set in, he would have to amputate Glenn's legs. He also said that there was not much he could do for Floyd. The two boys lay in their beds, talked and sang hymns, but seldom moved. On the ninth morning after the accident, Floyd died. Three months later, Glenn still could not move his legs or bend his knees, but his mother massaged his scarred limbs every day.

After six months had passed, Glenn's father put a big chair in the boy's room, and that chair became a brace and an exercise station. Each day, he pulled himself out of bed and held onto the sides of that chair and stretched and bent. On the day before Christmas, he told his mother that he had a Christmas present for her, but she had to stand by the door and close her eyes. She did so, and Glenn took a few faltering steps toward her. She reached out for him as they both slumped to the floor together.

By the next spring, his family had moved to another community, and Glenn had a two-mile walk to and from school. This exercise helped loosen his legs, but he still could not run without pain. Nevertheless, he kept trying. By the time he was twelve, he entered the school's track meet. All of the other boys were high school students, but Glenn wanted to compete with them anyway. He not only kept up with them but also passed them and won that race.

It was not the last race he would win. Glenn Cunningham went on to win an Olympic medal and to set world records for the eight hundred meters and the mile. He and his wife, Ruth, established the Cunningham Youth Ranch in Cedar Point, Kansas, where for thirty years they helped more than nine thousand troubled youths.[16]

What is the message in all of this? Never give up! Never quit! Never take "No" for an answer! Self-control means being master over yourself to the point of not allowing disappointments, and even tragedies, to deter you from your ultimate goals and dreams. God's power is available to His children to do anything in His will. As Paul put it, "I can do everything through him who gives me strength" (Phil. 4:13).

William Backus is the author of a book titled *Finding the Freedom of Self-Control*. He suggests several steps in learning self-control. First, take issues one at a time. If you have several problems on which to work, choose one that is most important and deal with it first. Then move on to the others. Second, begin to work on self-control issues with a prayer of repentance. Backus says, "Believe that God will, through Christ, not merely forgive your sins, but take them away and replace them with the self-control you need for change."[17] Next, use a self-control journal. In a small pocket notebook, record behavior that involves self-control issues. The reason? "Recording episodes of failure and success in the particular self-control area you are working on will allow you to see concrete evidence of change and improvement." Finally, do it now! Work on your issues when they arise instead of putting them off until later.

Dealing with Life

The fruit of the Spirit is . . . self-control.

This is an amazing statement. God wants His children to live above the level of physical cravings. He wants them to live intentionally, that is, to formulate principles and guidelines and goals for life, and then to follow them. Anything else brings trouble.

Proverbs 5:20–23 is a father's advice to his son to exercise self-control when it comes to women. The father says, "Why be captivated, my son, by an adulteress? Why embrace the bosom of another man's wife? For a man's ways are in full view of the LORD, and he examines all his paths. The evil deeds of a wicked man ensnare him; the cords of his sin hold him fast. *He will die for lack of discipline,* led astray by his own great folly" (italics added).

A friend of mine once told me about his early life. He had to get married because his girlfriend was pregnant. Their marriage was shaky from the start and ended in divorce. This friend later married again, and shortly before his wedding he told me something I will never forget: "You know, it's taken me a long time to learn, but I've finally decided to start thinking with my mind instead of with my sex organs." He had finally come to have this grace-gift of self-control in his life.

This aspect of the fruit of the Spirit allows you to cultivate talents, abilities, and insights that are uniquely yours and then to use those abilities for the cause of Christ. Each of us is as individual as our fingerprints. Each can do things that no one else can do in exactly the same way. I mentioned at the beginning of this chapter that self-control is not primarily negative, as in Archie Bunker's sense, "Stifle yourself!" Instead, this quality of discipline is positive because it allows us to focus our abilities instead of dissipate them. Ernest T. Campbell wrote a prayer thanking God for the unique gifts that various people have brought to the church. I close this chapter with this prayer and add to it my own "amen" because Campbell is right on target. May God grant us the courage to be self-controlled for His sake as well as our own.

> We bless Thee for Thy church,
>> one in the Holy Spirit
>> yet richly varied in its several parts.
> We remember in a single breath of gratitude:
>> The disciplined thought of Aquinas;
>> The care-free simplicity of St. Francis;
>> The raging discontent of Luther;
>> The expository gifts of Calvin;
>>> The prayer life of St. Theresa;
>>> The enthusiasm of the Wesleys;
>>> The pregnant silence of George Fox;
>>> The conscience of Leo Tolstoy;

The stirring utterances and courageous
   actions of Martin Luther King Jr.;
The poems of Marianne Moore;
The plays of T. S. Elliot;
The social vision of Camile Torres.
Add to Thy church in every place, O God,
   such as will love Thee with all their powers,
For we yearn to see embodied
   the kind of faith that can move mountains
   and set Thy people free.
Through Jesus Christ our Lord, Amen.[18]

Living in the Spirit, Walking in the Spirit

THIS BOOK HAS BEEN AN examination of Galatians 5:22, the fruit of the Spirit. Each element of the Spirit listed in that verse is one aspect of a well-rounded and balanced Christian life. Who could imagine, for example, such a life devoid of love or peace or patience? These are the basics for Christian living.

In the next two verses in Galatians, Paul has a little more to say about living in the Spirit: "Those who belong to Christ Jesus have crucified the sinful nature with its passions and desires. Since we live by the Spirit, let us keep in step with the Spirit." This is both a statement of theological truth and a request. What does Paul mean? In this last section, which I have called an epilogue, I want to look into Paul's meaning.

To "walk" in the Spirit means to live in, trust in, and act on what you know as the truth of God. It is continually to choose the way of spiritual life. It is to intermesh your life with the life of God so that you become sensitive to His presence. Malcolm Tolbert says, "The word *walk* encompasses attitudes, relationships, actions, goals—in short, all the way in which a person expresses his or her being."[1] He also states, "*Walk* . . . stands for conduct. The term embraces attitudes, acts, and relationships. The specific idea is related to the believer's life in the body of Christ."[2] To walk in the Spirit, then, is to develop an attitude and way of life that is sensitive to and quickened by the Spirit.

Some people try to live by the Law. The trouble with that is that the Law, as exemplified by an encoded tradition, is dead. Paul says in Romans 2:13–15 that such Law has no internal power over anyone. Other people try to live by the Ten Commandments. This is helpful but inadequate by itself. Paul notes in 2 Corinthians 3:12–13 that the power of the Ten Commandments alone, as delivered by Moses, has faded like the shine on Moses' face. The alternative to trying to live up to some external authority or guideline is to have an internal guide—the Spirit.

To walk in the Spirit is to experience the freedom that He gives. This is both freedom from and freedom for. It is freedom from the dominance of sin. It is also freedom for ethical and righteous living. George Appleton stated this idea thus: "Freedom in Christ is not freedom to do what I like, but freedom to be what I am meant to be. It is freedom from all the chains which hold me back from being my true self. It is freedom from all imposed limitations and external pressures. It is to share in Christ's freedom to do God's will, and then to help others find a similar freedom."[3]

The slogan "Be all that you can be" applies not only to the United States Army but also to the Christian army!

Someone is always wanting to control your life. You might as well come to grips with this fact. Even in the church I find people who want to control me and manipulate me, so I try to be sensitive not to do that to others. You see, the church is Christ's, not mine or yours. To live in the Spirit means that I surrender my life to no one except Christ. I cannot surrender my life to my spouse, my career, my children, my friends, or any other person.

This does not mean that I refuse to listen to them or shut them out emotionally. Far from it. I need my family and my friends. What I am referring to is the basic fact that I have only one life, and that many forces are pulling at it. Some of those forces are good, and some of them are not so good. Therefore, I must be very careful what or who I allow to influence me. This choosing is part of what living in the Spirit means.

To walk in the Spirit is also to experience a liberation that allows us to love others. This is absolutely basic. To love others is to invest ourselves in them. It is to allow them space and time for growth and change, even if that means that they grow away from us.

To walk in the Spirit is to remember that any of our perspectives are limited. Therefore, we must keep a proper humility about us. None of us knows it all and has life put together in a nice bundle. Even the apostle Paul realized his limitations. When the people in Corinth asked him about certain matters related to marriage, Paul responded with a word that he called his own (see 2 Cor. 7:25, 40). He could have spoken as if his opinion were the final authority. Instead, he told the Corinthians that his word on their question was his opinion and his personal judgment. He spoke with a sense of certainty but not unbending dogmatism. Let him who has ears hear!

A pastor of another generation used to say, "It's not how high you jump that counts, but how straight you walk when you come back down." There is a world of wisdom in this folksy proverb. Most of us can hit the stratosphere once in a while. It is our terrestrial ramblings that give us trouble. This is why we need to concentrate on the basics of Christian living.

My wedding ring has three words and three symbols on the outside of it. It has the word *Faith* with a cross, *Hope* with an anchor, and *Love* with a heart. These words and symbols help me remember who I am and what my commitments are. This is also true with the basics of the Spirit.

Godspeed to you as you try to incorporate the fruit of the Spirit in your life. My hope and prayer for you is that these aspects of spiritual life become living realities for you. During the next year, you might try to dedicate one month to each of the elements. Concentrate for thirty days on the meaning of love, and explore ways you can put it into practice. Then turn to joy, and so on.

May God bless you as you enjoy living by the fruit of the Spirit.

Endnotes

Introduction

1. Eugene Peterson, *The Contemplative Pastor,* The Leadership Library, vol. 17 (Dallas: Word, 1989), 42.
2. John Baillie, quoted in *Journey for a Soul,* by George Appleton (Glasgow: William Collins and Sons, 1974), 222.

Chapter 1

1. Dean Ornish, *Love & Survival: The Scientific Basis for the Healing Power of Intimacy* (New York: HarperCollins, 1998), 3.
2. *Baker Encyclopedia of Psychology,* s.v. "love," ed. David G. Banner (Grand Rapids: Baker, 1985).
3. Henry Drummond, *The Greatest Thing in the World.* This chart is from the edition by Lewis A. Drummond, *Love: The Greatest Thing in the World* (Grand Rapids: Kregel, 1998), 34.
4. Francis de Sales, "Living Selections from the Great Devotional Classics," in *Introduction to the Devout Life* (Nashville: Upper Room, 1962), 14.
5. Dorothy and Thomas Hoobler, "Joseph Stalin," in *World Leaders Past and Present* (New York: Chelsea House, 1985), 25.
6. Stuart Miller, *Men and Friendship* (Boston: Houghton Mifflin, 1983), 2.
7. Ibid., 191.
8. For more on this, see my book *God's Man: Daily Devotions for Christlike Character* (Grand Rapids: Kregel, 1998).

9. Augustine, quoted in *The Wisdom of the Body,* by Sherwin B. Nuland (New York: Alfred A. Knopf, 1997), unnumbered flyleaf.

10. Evelyn Eaton Whitehead and James D. Whitehead, *Christian Life Patterns: The Psychological Challenges and Religious Invitations of Adult Life* (Garden City, N.Y.: Doubleday, 1979), 43–44.

11. Thomas Lea, *Galatians: Saved by Grace* (Nashville: Convention, 1994), 107.

12. Margery Williams, *The Velveteen Rabbit* (Philadelphia: Running, 1981), 14–15. Used by permission of the publisher.

Chapter 2

1. William Morrice, *Joy in the New Testament* (Grand Rapids: Eerdmans, 1984.)

2. Mother Teresa, quoted in Eileen Egan and Kathleen Egan, eds., *Suffering into Joy: What Mother Teresa Teaches about True Joy* (Ann Arbor: Servant, 1994), 38.

3. Bill Hybels with Rob Wilkins, *Descending into Greatness* (Grand Rapids: Zondervan, 1993), 181.

4. John Wesley, "Selections from the Journal of John Wesley," arr. and ed. Paul Lambourned Higgins, *Living Selections from the Great Devotional Classics* (Nashville: Upper Room, 1967), 26.

5. Christiaan N. Barnard, "In Celebration of Being Alive," *Reader's Digest,* April 1980, 16. Used by permission of the author.

6. Henri J. M. Nouwen, *The Wounded Healer* (Garden City, N.Y.: Image, 1979), 84. Used by permission.

7. Eugene H. Peterson, *The Contemplative Pastor: Returning to the Art of Spiritual Direction* (Dallas: Word, 1989), 13–14.

8. W. R. Inge, quoted in *A Treasury of the Kingdom,* comp. E. A. Blackburn and others (New York: Oxford University Press, 1954), 127.

9. L. D. Johnson, *Moments of Reflection* (Nashville: Broadman, 1980), 47.

10. W. B. Wolfe, quoted in *Speaker's Illustrations for Special Days,* ed. Charles L. Wallis (New York: Abingdon, 1956), 164.

11. Louis Evely, *Joy,* trans. Brian and Marie-Claude Thompson

(New York: Herder and Herder, 1968), 9.

Chapter 3

1. Story by James O'Byrne, *The Times-Picayune/The States Item,* September 17, 1985, A-17 and A-18.
2. Editorial by Lynn P. Clayton, *Baptist Message,* 31 October 1985, 4.
3. Told by P. L. Garlick in *A Treasury of the Kingdom,* comp. E. A. Blackburn (New York: Oxford University Press, 1954), 120–21.
4. Ann Morrow Lindbergh, *Gift from the Sea,* rev. ed. (New York: Pantheon, 1975), 23.
5. Dave Grossman, cited in a front page story, *Baptist Message,* 20 August 1998.
6. This story is about Louise Degrafinred and Riley Arceneaux, *The Commercial Appeal,* 20 August 1998, A-16.
7. Kenneth S. Kantzer, editorial, *Christianity Today,* 13 December 1985, 18.
8. William J. Shaw, "From Shells into Bells," *The Student,* December 1985, 44.

Chapter 4

1. Martin Groder, "The Power of Strategic Waiting," *Bottom Line,* 1 October 1997, 17.
2. J. I. Packer, "A Bad Trip," *Christianity Today,* 16 March 1986, 12.
3. William Barclay, *Flesh and Spirit: An Examination of Galatians 5:19–23* (Grand Rapids: Baker, 1976 [1962]), 96. (Italics mine.)
4. Bill Galston, quoted in "Get a Life," by Michael Warshaw, *Fast Company,* June–July 1998, 140.
5. Reuters story, "Study: Anger Raises Heart Disease Risk," *The Commercial Appeal,* 1 November 1996, A-5.
6. John Davies, *Good News in Galatians* (Cleveland: Collins/World Publishing, 1975), 92.
7. Chrysostom, quoted in *A Treasury of the Kingdom,* comp. E. A. Blackburn, (New York: Oxford University Press, 1954), 144–45.
8. Rodney Clapp, "Laboratories of the Soul," *Christianity Today,* 7 March 1986, 26.
9. Don Honig, quoted in "The Man Pete Rose Chased—And

Caught," by Furman Bisher, *Sky,* November 1985, 124.

10. This ancient story is found in the *Talmud,* a Jewish commentary, and is retold several places, notably in the book by William B. Silverman, *Rabbinic Stories for Christian Ministers and Teachers* (Nashville: Abingdon, 1953), 88–89.

Chapter 5

1. Paul Tudor Jones, *The Chain of Kindness* (Little Rock: August House, 1992), 168.
2. Morton Hunt, quoted in *The Joy of Kindness,* by Robert J. Furey (New York: Crossroads, 1993), 5.
3. Oscar Wilde, quoted in *Creative Brooding,* by Robert Raines (New York: Collier, 1966), 86. (Italics mine.)
4. Gerald Kennedy, *Second Reader's Notebook* (New York: Harper and Brothers, 1954), 200.
5. Associated Press story, *Lake Charles American Press,* 29 October 1993, 31.
6. Gavin Whitsett, *Guerrilla Kindness* (San Luis Obispo, Calif.: Impact, 1993), 7.
7. R. Dass and Paul Gorman, *How Can I Help? Stories and Reflections on Service* (New York: Alfred A. Knopf, 1985), 54.
8. Furey, *Joy of Kindness,* 95–96.
9. Aletha Jane Lindstrom, "A Legacy of Rainbows," *Focus on the Family,* April 1986, 12–13.

Chapter 6

1. Helen Waddell, *The Desert Fathers,* cited in *A Treasury of the Kingdom,* comp. E. A. Blackburn (New York: Oxford University Press, 1954), 167–68.
2. Cited by Alan Loy McGinnis, *The Friendship Factor* (Minneapolis: Augsburg, 1979), 15.
3. The word that is translated *goodness* in Galatians 5:22 is *agatosuna* in Greek. It means generosity as well as goodness. *A Greek-English Lexicon of the New Testament and Other Early Christian Literature,* 4th ed., trans. and ed. W. F. Arndt and F. W. Gingrich (Chicago: University of Chicago Press, 1957), 3.

4. Spencer Marsh, *God, Man, and Archie Bunker* (New York: Bantam, 1975), 14–16.
5. Quoted in *The Interpreter's Bible,* vol. 11 (New York: Abingdon, 1954), 94.
6. Dietrich Bonhoeffer, quoted in *An End to Innocence: Facing Life Without Illusions,* by Sheldon Kopp (New York: Bantam, 1981 [1978]), 112.
7. Sheldon Kopp, *If You Meet the Buddha on the Road, Kill Him!* (New York: Bantam, 1976 [1972]), 193.
8. Herman Melville, quoted in *The Interpreter's Bible,* vol. 11 (New York: Abingdon, 1955), 94.
9. Albert Schweitzer, *Out of My Life and Thought: An Autobiography,* trans. C. T. Campion (New York: New American Library, 1953 [1933]), 73.
10. Paul Tournier, *Creative Suffering,* trans. Edwin Hudson (San Francisco: Harper and Row, 1982), 94–95.

Chapter 7

1. William Barclay, *Flesh and Spirit* (Grand Rapids: Baker, 1976 [1962]), 107–8.
2. Ibid., 111.
3. This anonymous prayer is from an article by Anita Deyneka, "God in the Gulag," *Christianity Today,* 9 August 1985, 31.
4. Flannery O'Connor, quoted by Paul W. Nisly, "Faith Is Not an Electric Blanket," *Christianity Today,* 17 May 1985, 24.
5. Dietrich Bonhoeffer, *Selections from the Writing of Dietrich Bonhoeffer,* arr. and ed. Orlo Strunk Jr., *Living Selections from the Great Devotional Classics* (Nashville: Upper Room, 1967), 12.
6. Calvin Coolidge, quoted by Henry W. Foster Jr. with Alice Greenwood, *Make a Difference* (New York: Scribner, 1997), 184.
7. Armstrong Williams, quoted in *The Miracle of Change: The Path to Self-Discovery and Spiritual Growth,* by Dennis Wholey (New York: Pocket Books, 1997), 151.
8. Doug McCray, "Death Watch: A Journal by Doug McCray," *The Plough,* May–June 1986, 17. This interview originally

appeared in the book by Dough Magee, *Slow Coming Dark* (New York: Pilgrim, 1980).

9. If you are troubled by anger at someone, you might deal with it in this helpful way. Psychologist Alan Loy McGinnis suggests five techniques to help deal with anger. First, talk about your feelings, not about your friend's faults. Second, stick to the one topic at hand. Third, allow your friend to respond. Fourth, aim for ventilation, not conquest. Fifth, balance criticism with a lot of affection. See chapter 13 of McGinnis's book *The Friendship Factor* (Minneapolis: Augsburg, 1979).

10. Lewis B. Smedes, "Controlling the Unpredictable: The Power of Promising," *Christianity Today,* 21 January 1983, 16–19.

11. Maltbie D. Babcock, *Treasury of Courage and Confidence,* abridg. and ed. Norman Vincent Peale (Anderson, Ind.: Warner, 1974), 75.

12. Royalties from books are usually not very large. A Columbia University study of 2,239 authors found that the average writer earned only $4,774 per year—hardly enough on which to live. See the book that I wrote with Len Goss, *The Christian Writers Book* (Plainfield, N.J.: Bridge-Logos, 1996).

Chapter 8

1. William Barclay, *Flesh and Spirit* (Grand Rapids: Baker, 1976 [1962]), 121.

2. Phil Barnhart, *Seasonings for Sermons* (Lima, Ohio: C.S.S., 1980), 77.

3. Sheldon Vanauken, *A Severe Mercy* (New York: Bantam, 1979 [1977]), 88.

4. Malcolm O. Tolbert, *Ephesians: God's New People* (Nashville: Convention, 1979), 89.

5. Martin Bennett, "Walking in Weakness the Path of the Mighty," *The Last Days Magazine* 9, no. 1 (1986): 11.

6. William Barclay, *Letters to Galatians and Ephesians,* Daily Study Bible (Edinburgh: Saint Andrews Press, 1954), 56–57.

7. Thomas à Kempis, quoted in *Disciplines for the Inner Life,* by Bob Benson, Sr. and Michael W. Benson (Nashville: Nelson, 1989), 103.

8. Francis de Sales, *Selections from the Introduction to the Devout Life,* arr. and ed. Thomas S. Kepler, *Living Selections from the Great Devotional Classics* (Nashville: Upper Room, 1962), 23–24.

9. These recollections of Johnson are recounted in Barclay, *Flesh and Spirit,* 113.

10. Scott Alexander, *Rhinoceros Success* (Laguna Hills, Calif.: Rhino's Press, 1980), 11.

11. Floyd Patterson, quoted in "The Sanctification of Sport: Can the Mind of Christ Coexist with the Killer Instinct?" by Shirl J. Hoffman, *Christianity Today,* 4 April 1986, 18.

12. Interview with Pete Maravich in *The Bogalusa Daily News,* 19 May 1986, 10.

13. Charles Kingsley, quoted in *The Interpreter's Bible,* vol. 4 (New York: Abingdon, 1954), 896.

14. St. Teresa, from *The Way of Perfection* and *The Foundations,* in *A Treasury of the Kingdom,* comp. E. A. Blackburn (New York: Oxford University Press, 1954), 197.

Chapter 9

1. *The Westminster Dictionary of Christian Theology,* s.v. "Discipline," ed. Alan Richardson and John Bowden (Philadelphia: Westminster Press, 1983).

2. Morgan Phelps Noyes, *The Interpreter's Bible,* vol. 11 (New York: Abingdon, 1955), 537.

3. Abraham Heschel, quoted by Bob Benson Sr. and Michael W. Benson, *Disciplines for the Inner Life* (Nashville: Nelson, 1989), 163.

4. Evelyn Eaton Whitehead and James D. Whitehead, *Christian Life Patterns: The Psychological Challenges and Religious Invitations of Adult Life* (Garden City: Doubleday, 1979), 44.

5. Bob Thaves, *Frank & Ernest,* 30 March 1998.

6. Larry Crabb, "Self-Control," *Discipleship Journal,* no. 44 (1988): 20.

7. John Erskine, quoted in *The Psychology of Winning,* by Denis Waitley (New York: Berkley, 1984 [1979]), 51.

8. Ibid., 122–23.

9. S. Parkes Cadman, *Imagination* (New York: E. P. Dutton, 1930), 84. See also his *Imagination and Religion* (New York: Macmillan, 1926).

10. Waitley, *Psychology of Winning*, 51.

11. Phillips P. Elliott, *The Interpreter's Bible*, vol. 2 (New York: Abingdon, 1953), 744–45.

12. John Davies, *Good News in Galatians* (Cleveland: Collins/World Publishing, 1975), 93.

13. Rolland W. Schloerb, *The Interpreter's Bible*, vol. 4 (New York: Abingdon, 1954), 878.

14. Carl G. Jung, *Modern Man in Search of a Soul* (New York: Harcourt, Brace, and Co., 1933), 211.

15. Booker T. Washington, *Up from Slavery* (New York: Lancer, 1968 [1901]), 24–25.

16. Glenn Cunningham's story is told in his autobiography, *Never Quit* (Lincoln, Va.: Chosen, 1981).

17. William Backus, *Finding the Freedom of Self-Control* (Minneapolis: Bethany House, 1987), 49.

18. Ernest T. Campbell, *Campbell's Notebook* 5, no. 1, 3. Used by permission of the author.

Epilogue

1. Malcolm O. Tolbert, *Ephesians: God's New People* (Nashville: Convention, 1979), 37.

2. Ibid., 106.

3. George Appleton, *Journey for a Soul* (Glasgow: William Collins and Sons, 1974), 181.